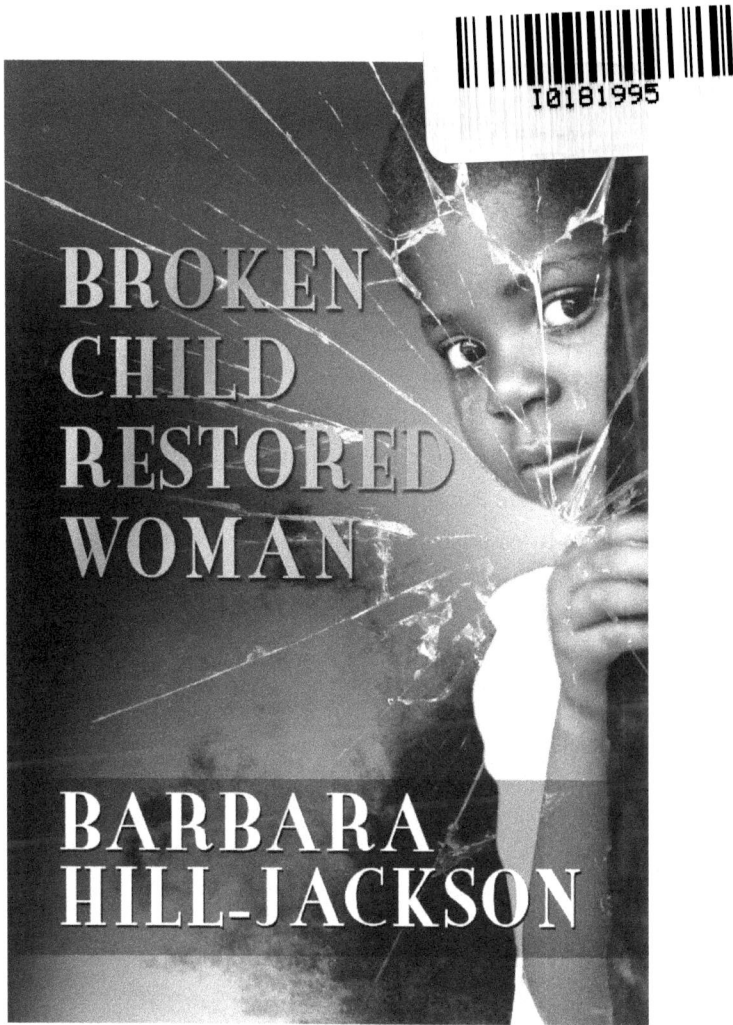

BROKEN CHILD RESTORED WOMAN

Copyright @2014 by Barbara Hill-Jackson

ISBN 978-0-692-2602-3

Jackson Publishing

Cover Design: VC Custom Designs; Tamikaink.com

All rights reserved solely by the Author. No part of this book may be reproduced in any form without the permission of the author. The Author guarantees all contents are original and do not infringe upon the legal right of any other person or work.

PRINTED IN THE UNITED STATES

www.restoredwoman.com

HOUSTON, TEXAS 77047

Barbara knew what it felt like to be a broken child. To be sick with guilt, worry, shame, fear, thoughts of suicide and wanting to kill her abuser. This ate at her very soul, she couldn't tell, and she couldn't leave. Going to school every day weighed heavily but the one thing that Barbara wanted most of all was for her mother to have enough courage to leave and never return, only if this was possible. The pain and scars were never seen in the eyes of others, but each day looking into the mirror she knew that the pain and the scars would one day be no more. Barbara somehow learned to live with the abuse, tolerate the pain, and protect her mother at all cost – even if she had to take the abuse herself.

My mother wasn't strong enough to leave, she stayed out of fear. Her fear being if she left him he would one day find and kill her not realizing that if she stayed the beatings would eventually kill her slowly. Either way death haunted my mother greatly. If I had to do it all over again, I would have taken my mother and never looked back. I would have gotten her the help that she needed to overcome the low self-esteem and the courage to fight back. All of the drugs, the parties, the nude night clubs, pushed my mother into a world that she had grown accustomed to by the hands of my step-father, she did only out of fear. As a child I watched my mother fall into a lifestyle that she didn't have any intentions on living or exposing my sister, brother and I too. In spite of it all, mother still loved us.

BROKEN CHILD RESTORED WOMAN

-Table of Contents-

Acknowledgments...	8
Dedication...	9
Preface...	11
Introduction	13
Poem – "Please Love Stop Hurting Me"	14
Chapter 1 - Exposed To Soon	15
Chapter 2 – Fearful, Worried and Abused	27
Chapter 3 - The Night It All Began...........................	33
Poem: "Stranger in my room"	33
Chapter 4 - Running Away To Be Safe.......................	41
Chapter 5 - 16-Pregnant and Married........................	53
Poem- "Trusting God in Singlehood"........................	63
Chapter 6 - Repeating the Cycle with Hidden Fears.........	65
Poem: "Writing for the Cure"......................	70
Chapter 7 - Living free, Now Restored............	79
Prayer...	89
Poem- "Restored"..	91
About the Author..	92
Question- Why Did I Stay?.......................................	94

> Broken - break (verb)
> Fractured, not in working order violated as a vow, interrupted imperfectly spoken, tamed.
> Being broken does not mean that a person will never be able to press beyond all the brokenness in their life it just means that you may have been violated or interrupted.
> Have you ever been watching TV and there was an interruption in the program that you were watching.
> It says please stay tuned this is an interruption in the regular scheduled program and it will resume shortly.

This is what often happens to us in our lives, sometimes we have interruptions, but there is good news. When you are broken you can be put back together again, interruptions will come but you will be back on the right path shortly. As I think back on what happened to me I thought being broken was a permanent place. What I did not know was that my pain would one day help and bless others. There are many things in life that cannot be fixed, but matters of the heart, mind, spirit, and emotions can be repaired. In ones' life journey there will be things, people, and circumstances that will either break your heart or break your spirit but in all you will be restored from it.

When you have experienced being broken it is not a very good feeling. When you are broken it seems as if everything around you is broken or breaking you down. You may even feel like you will never find that place of peace and total healing, but you will make it through no matter what has happened to you. Just read "Broken Child Restored Woman," you will be restored. One should never flee from ones fears but embrace them and work through them.

A WORD OF THANKS

I would like to thank my pastor, **Dr. Charles Perry Jr.** and **First Lady Charlette Perry**. The two have been a blessing in my life in many ways. When I think about all that I went through being broken as a child it makes me appreciate the life I now live. At the time I came to The Word of Restoration International Church I was in so much pain and disbelief but I knew one day I would be restored through their teachings. My sister, Cornelia Coleman invited me to attend the service. Each Sunday it seemed that all of the messages were only for me. I began to apply the words that Pastor Perry and First Lady spoke into my life – oh how my life began to take shape and form. I started to release all the pain of being broken as a child; I began to forgive myself and my stepfather.

I never knew what it really meant to be free until I started to feel God's presence in my life and things started shifting for the better. I recall one Sunday Pastor Perry's lesson was, "Breaking Generational Curses." I left church that Sunday and I went home got into my prayer closet and wept like never before. I asked God to show me His glory and what I was supposed to be doing now that I was in my early fifties. I knew that I was struggling with the strongholds in my life and needed the curse to be broken over my life and the lives of my children. I wanted and desired to be free so that God could use me to be a blessing for others. There were many teachings; along with the words that were spoken into my life that helped me overcome and find my purpose in life. There are no words to express how grateful I am to have my spiritual leaders.

BARBARA HILL-JACKSON

    I can truly say, "To God Be the Glory," for this great ministry. I admire and praise God for Pastor and First Lady. Pastor, thank you so much for bringing Prophet Joseph Hargo to the church. On September 8, 2013, just like He spoke a word into your life many years ago, he spoke a word into my life on that day. The word was, "Half-Way There, Halfway to loosing, No, Halfway to Winning." My life has never been the same since I have been a member at The Word of Restoration International Church. Pastor, thank you once again for empowering me with the word of God that helped me to become a restored woman.

                                Love, Barbara Jackson

-*Acknowledgments*-

Writing this book was by far one of the hardest things in my life to do. I knew in writing this I would revisit those dark places of what happened to me as a young girl. I knew that I had to tell my story. Not just for me to be free from all of the guilt, hurt, shame, fear, anxiety, worry, depression, thoughts of killing myself and my abuser. The things that he did to me kept me paralyzed for so many years. I write for all those girls, for my sisters all over the land letting you know that I'm here for you. I embrace and share with you your pain and this book is not just for me to tell my story, but to help you press past your pain. The freedom that you hold is far better than holding on to what has happened or what is happening to you. Visit speakyoursilence.org; stopitnow.org; or childabuse.org. There is someone that you can tell and that will listen.

I appreciate the encouragement that I have received from those that have walked with me through my journey in writing this book. There are those that I had called on and they would take time to listen to some of the writings that I shared leading up to the publishing of my book.

Special Thanks to: Mrs. Cornelia Coleman (sister), Ms. Meche Hart, Mrs. Kim Daniels, Mr. Leon Johnson, Mr. Charles O'Saw, Mr. Rodney Woods, Mr. Pha Green, Mrs. Patricia Porter, Mrs. Shirley Johnson, Mr. Charles Mitchell, Ms. Martha Kelly, Ms. Jackie Jammer, Ms. Mary Smith, Mr. and Mrs. Karel Bell, Sr., Mrs. Melba Mitchell, Mr. Allen Wilson, Ms. Angela Cobbs-Cooper and Ms. Desarie Steadman.

-Dedication-

It is my prayer that every sister that reads this book understands that no matter what your background, career, occupation, color of your skin, level of education, religion, or familial status there is help beyond what you are going through or have been through. This may or may not be your story, but there is someone that you know that has experienced some form of abuse in their lives.

You are my sister because I have walked in your shoes, so my prayer is that when you finish reading this book it will bless you, restore, heal and help you to overcome all those things that have been keeping you from taking a stand and finding that place where healing may begin. It is my desire that healing will meet you in the dark places of your life, where all the pain, guilt, worry, and fear are stored. If I was able to do so it would be my hope to personally escort you to your place of restoration.

You can overcome all the pain, guilt and shame that you have been holding onto for so many years. It is not God's will for anyone to live in fear, guilt, shame and abuse to be overtaken by their past. This keeps them from living for the present while looking forward to their future. I lived this way for many years, this is why I have decided to write this book to reach all those that have gone; and that are going through what I have. God clearly said that it is not His will that anyone should perish.

I think that fear paralyzes the mind, body and soul of a person, keeping them from being what God has called them to be. Fear keeps you locked up and connected to the past. As mighty Women of God we must hold on to the truth that has been given to us by our Heavenly Father and not the lies from satan.

So take hold of the gifts that are within, expand the visions and dreams that can be reached by letting go of the past, because it is no longer part of your tomorrow.

I dedicate this book to the loving memory of my mother, Emma Kathryn Gregory Robinson, and my grandmother, Rosa Leona Moore Gregory.

Emma Kathryn Gregory Robinson, gone too soon loved ever so much.

-Preface-

Riding a bike, fear of falling, frogs, snakes, scary movies, high roller coaster rides, and stormy weather was not so scary for me as a young girl. However, there was one thing that I was afraid of the most and that was going to sleep at night. I would clinch my teeth, rock, shake and cry every night before I would go to bed, you ask why; because of the horrible things that happened to me as a child. I could not tell and when I did tell, no one believed me. They said I was making up everything and causing trouble.

I would rock in the middle of the floor when I was a young girl. No one knew but my mother's sister said, "Something is wrong with Barbara, it's not normal for a child to do what she is doing. Something is troubling her."

Traumatized as a kid, the stress, pain, and abuse came out in many different ways. I guess this was my way of letting my family know that something was really wrong. There were some days I would even faint and I was hospitalized for testing. The doctors could not find any health problems, but inside I was hurting and in pain. All I knew was that I wanted the pain to stop. My spirit was crying out, "Listen, you will not find anything wrong with my health! It's mental!"

I think any form of abuse is unhealthy for anyone at any age. In those days they did not question children like they do today to see if there has been any sexual abuse. If they would have questioned me they would have uncovered the real truth about what was going on in my house and the sexual abuse I endured.

Through it all, I thank the Lord because in spite of the sexual, mental and physical abuse I did not resort to drugs or alcohol. I did not concede to the lifestyle that I was exposed to at such an early age. Somehow I knew that the Lord had His hands on me and a much better plan for my life. In writing this book I have released my pain and sadness so that I may be free of all the things that I held onto for so many years. I still reflect back on those horrible things only to be reminded of the new me and being thankful of the life I now live. I have become stronger and know that it was the Lord that brought me out of all those dark places in my life. I had to grow up very fast as a child, that was stressful in itself and to deal with the abuse I went through was painful. Seeing my mother abused was even harder for me. As a child, I was not able to process all of the horror. I acted out in many different ways. As I matured in life it was my faith and trust in God that helped me become better.

-Introduction-

Several years ago I was going through a very unsustainable relationship, where I found myself lied to and cheated on. It was so overwhelming to me that I would spend countless hours crying and trying to find all the answers as to why I allowed this man to have so much control over my emotions. This is when it all became clear to me that I was repeating the same cycle that I had experienced in my childhood. I saw my mother let a certain man have control over her life.

Knowing what I had gone through in this bad relationship brought back painful memories of me being abused as a child and watching my mother being abused. No matter where I find myself; just knowing the Lord will heal any type of hurt strengthens me. He provides strength to endure through the journey and restores anyone to embrace their future. Below is a poem that I wrote that helped me during my healing process:

BROKEN CHILD RESTORED WOMAN

PLEASE LOVE STOP HURTING ME

Please love, stop hurting me

Come close and listen to the words I have to say about the love I thought I had that just up and walked away
If you could look into my heart and see why I'm so sad you will see that I have been hurt by love really bad.

I'm not a woman that's bitter mad or scorn
I'm just going through my healing when my heart has been torn.
I may be partially the blame when the love I gave was not reciprocated the same

I know that love has its ups and it downs
I'm not going to give up on love because I know it will be found.

I want a love that will be there through thick and through thin
A love in whom I can always depend
I want a love that's really great a love that I know that's my soul mate

Please love stop hurting me I want to experience real love that is faithful and honest you see

I know that in love we will take chances and risk
I want a love that I know was heaven sent.
I don't want love to hurt me anymore
I don't want a love that's just looking to score
Please love stop hurting me, can't you see what you're doing to me
You see I don't want to attract any more wrong men in my life
I want love in a man who finds me and makes me his wife.

By Barbara Jackson
October 2012

CHAPTER 1
-Exposed Too Soon-

> EXPOSED - To lay open to danger, attack, harm, etc.

My grandmother would tell me, "Baby do not take a bath and go outside right away because your pores are still open and you are exposing yourself to catching a cold. Put something on your head and some socks on your feet." She was teaching me not to expose myself to the elements that will eventually make me sick. This is what I went through exposed too soon as a child by what I had seen, and it made me sick with guilt, fear, shame, worry, and anger.

I remember as a young girl we would move more than the average family. I know they say that change is good for the soul, well this young soul had enough of changing and moving. When you have too many unexplained changes in your life as a child you have a tendency to be somewhat withdrawn and disconnected in your own way. Whether you want to call it exposed, introduced, seen, or lived, it is all the same. I know that my mother never intended for us to go through what we went through and let us see what we had seen in our lives. Most parents conceal and cover up things from their children so that they will not worry and that their behavior will not change. There are a lot of children living in abusive households. The unfortunate thing is that when the child starts having trouble in school if the abuse is not discovered it can be really damaging.

I remember the long night's mother stayed away from home. I recall not being able to figure out when mother would ever come home, and all the fights that mother would have with our stepfather. The fights caused me to worry and it kept me in fear.

All the fighting, drugs, mental and physical abuse that you have to see a love one go through is really hard when you are a child and trying to understand the reason why. I did research and found out that in a household, nine out of 10 people that live in an abusive household will repeat the same cycle in the same or similar way. They will become an abuser themselves, marry an abuser, or be in a relationship that threatens the safety of the people living there. All the while seeing that being happy and wholesome is somewhat out of their reach.

When I was a little girl I loved watching fairy tales, love stories, and movies with happy families. This is what I would wish for and wanted in my family. We had all of this until my stepfather came into the picture. You see, my biological father was an alcoholic and he abused my mother from what I can remember. Mother went from my dad abusing her to my stepfather abusing her.

We started out as a big happy family with a very nice apartment where my mother, brother, sister and I lived on the Southeast side of town. It was not the best but my mother made it our little home. We lived there for many years it was called "the projects", I must say it was our home and it was filled with our mother's love. She would work hard each and every day. I never heard her complain, but yet I could tell by watching, she was very tired. She worked two jobs. I think her favorite job was Dr. Pepper although Pepsi was her favorite soda. She would ride the bus to both of her jobs or catch a ride from my aunts and uncles. Each and every night mother made sure dinner was on the table and we did our homework. We had so much fun together as a family, especially on Sundays after church when we would go over to my Aunt Barbara's (my namesake) and have dinner.

On Saturdays, we would have family breakfast with my aunt and uncle. My father was never around and when he did come around he was always drunk. We did not worry about getting any love from him because he did not show love. After he and mother split up, father over-indulged in his alcohol, he stayed drunk most of the times and would beat mother too. As a little girl I wished they would work it out but I knew mother was afraid of him. She did not want him around because whenever he was it was really bad, there was constant fighting, drinking, loud cursing and he would treat mother so bad.

We would have birthday parties and mother would dress my sister and me alike, and invite our friends over to have ice cream and cake to celebrate. We had lots of fun playing games like pin-the-tail-on-the-donkey. As the months and years passed I noticed that mother would get home later and later. I began to worry because this was not like mother – she would always be home for dinner and to check our homework. One night, mother came home very late and I could tell she did not have a good day. I asked her and she told me that she was so tired. This was the first time I had ever heard mother complain. She went on to say she was so unhappy because life was too hard for her trying to raise us with very little. I told her it would get better. We hugged and kissed, then, mother and I went to bed.

The next day mother was really late and we did not have food prepared for us. So I opened a can of corn and pork-n-beans. My sister, brother and I ate. After this, mother arriving late became the norm for us. It was hard for me to watch things change so very quickly and to have to care for my small sister and older brother. I was their surrogate mother. We had a neighbor, her name was Ms. Queenie. She and mother were really good friends and she watched out for us and mother watched out for her kids. The nights that mother would be late I would ask Ms. Queenie had she heard from her and when she would tell me no, my heart would drop. I did not know what was wrong or what may have happened to mother. One night I stayed awake and waited by the door hoping that she would come home. Hours passed but still no sign of her. I remember thinking to myself, "what would make mother stay away from home all night? Is she dead or hurt?" I did not know what it would be, but I knew it was something.

I was too young to know what to do for my brother and sister, but somehow I managed to make do with the responsibilities that I was forced to take on. As a child all I wanted was is to be a child. I did not want to have to take my mothers' place seeing all the things that she went through and was going through. I knew that the shoes that she wore were much too large for me to wear and I had no intentions of wearing them or taking her place. Often times I felt like a surrogate mother not a child, left with the responsibilities of raising my sister and brother was so hard. I was too young. If I had to do it all over again, I would because they mean the world to me and I wanted to make sure they were always safe.

The next morning I got up early to go outside to look for mother and to my surprise she was sitting in a yellow cab with a man I had never seen before. She told me to get in the cab, but I just turned and walked away. I went back upstairs and checked on my brother and sister to make sure they were still asleep so if mother decided not to come into the home they would not worry. However, soon mother entered the home and this man was sitting in our home. Somehow as a kid I knew he was not good for the family. Eventually, he was always around. When he would come around I would say my prayers at night asking God to make him disappear. I can recall him bringing lots and lots of things into our apartment that we never had before.

So many times in our lives we tend to be withdrawn and go into dark places where guilt, fear, shame and neglect resides. When love or a love one leaves us, cuts off the relationship, whether they die or for whatever the reason, it does not feel good to us. This is the way I was feeling as a child. I felt like my mother was leaving us and that he was tearing our family apart and our family would experience great pain, and trouble down the road.

I wanted my mother there with me all of the time because I had seen her go through so much and wanted her to be safe and happy. Her not coming home at night kept me scared leaving us all alone and me to care for my brother and sister.

I remember mother walking us to school and me not wanting her to leave us there. I wanted her to stay, because I was thinking about this strange man that had come into our family and boy he was bad news. I mean really bad news. I also remember attacking my teacher with my lunch box. Keep in mind back then those days lunch boxes were made out of tin, needless to say my teacher had many bruises.

At times I had to be strong while sometimes angry at mother because she allowed this man to come into our home and tear it apart. She continued to stay gone long hours, sometimes all night, and leaving me to care for the entire house. You may ask how I maintained the household. When you have a special strength that you are born with you can do anything. I knew that I had inherited a strength that was given to me from a higher source. I would need this strength later on in my life and for my life.

In my mind all I wanted was the day to end and mother to be standing outside my classroom door. Oh, what a relief it was to find her standing there when the door opened. As time moved on all of the days after school mother walked us home. We were together again as a family, especially when we got home and that man was not there. I thought he was gone but one evening while we were eating dinner, there was a knock at the door and there he was once again. Unsuspectingly, he was against the family and eventually caused our family nothing but pain. I asked myself if mother could see he is not good for her, heck even my father could see this drunk or sober.

I recall one time the man and my dad having words. My dad told him that he did not like and did not want him around. I really did not know who was the best person to have around, my father being drunk and abusive or that man coming in our little family to cause turmoil. Well, I guess every person has their own demons to deal with.

One particular day when I was seven years old my uncle picked us up from school. I knew something was wrong, where was mother? When my uncle would pick us up we would have to wave through a window once we were inside. On this day, I walked through the house before waving and I called out to mother. I looked everywhere and still could not find her. I opened the bathroom door and there she was laying on the floor, next to her an empty bottle of pills. I began to scream, "Mother! Mother! Oh my God, what has this man done to you? Mother, please, please wake up! Please open your eyes!"

I was too young to lose my mother like this and to be exposed to this was heart breaking for us. All I know I was determined to make sure that she did not die. What was I supposed to do? My siblings and I were not prepared for this. In today's world it is different, children learn CPR and so many other things, back then we didn't know this. I remember calling out, "Mother, mother! please mother just open your eyes say something," but mother just lay there as if life had left her body.

I ran outside to my uncle and said, "Please, please you have got to come help her she's not breathing and she won't open her eyes!"

I remember it like it was yesterday, he put mother in the tub and ran water all over her, took off his shoe and placed it over her nose this is when mother begin to come around. He called her name and slapped her face to get her to respond. Mother opened her eyes I guess you can say the Lord was not ready for her. From that day on the family was at our home every day watching out for mother, my sister, my brother and I. They knew mother needed help and as a family they helped.

In our family if someone was in need or if someone died, family came to help until matters were better. There were times when my aunts and grandmother would just help someone no matter what the situation. The man saw this and I guess it was getting too crowded because of all of the help after my mom's suicide attempt he stayed away for a few weeks.

Many years passed as mother continued to date this man, one day mother came to us to say that we were moving and that he had found a much nicer place for us to live. Moving? I had no idea where this home was except it was on the other side of town far away from my grandmother, my aunts and uncle. This was really bad and frightened me. We packed our things and loaded them in his car. When the car was loaded with our things we started driving down the road I began to cry. My heart was beating fast as I looking out of the window at the apartment where we used to live. Once we arrived at our new place we walked in and to my surprise my sister, brother and I had our own rooms. My mother and that man had a bigger room. I tried to feel happy about the change but I could not. You must keep in mind by this time I had seen and experienced a lot of adult things and exposed too soon to other things. I guess you can say this man had planned everything out.

The very next week my mother and he gave a big party. Those ladies wore some of the shortest dresses and the men had on some of the biggest hats, maybe it was the right fashion for that year. But, as children we didn't need to see some of the things that those people did when they came to our house but we did. Later on that night, my mother was sound asleep and my stepdad walked around the apartment wearing nothing but women's underwear. I went to my room and closed the door. The next day I told mother what happened and she let him know not to do this again.

As a child I was asking, "How could she allow him to even stay knowing what he did?" Oh I guess it was his place after all. Thinking back now that I am an adult if this was my child I would have put him out the first time; there would not have been a second chance for him at all. Every weekend there were parties and we never had family time. The parties would get out of hand. Not only were there drugs and unheard of things, but they would invite us into the parties. I began to call that man, "Mister."

Mister had a brother and when he would come to the parties he would have more drugs and more women. I did not like this man at all. One thing I did not like was when he would come over to visit he would ask me to sit in his lap and say, "I'm your new uncle." What kind of grown man would ask a young girl to sit on his lap? He was up to no good. I told my mother about what happened all she would say is, "He was just being himself and he did not mean any harm," but the harm was already done.

Now that this man was part of our lives we moved from one place to another and we weren't stable as a happy family anymore. He would bark orders and my mother would do just what he said not giving it a second thought. It amazes me how a person can have that much control over another person. The sad part about it he was not my father.

One day, I had walk to the laundromat to do the family laundry where my mother met me. As I began to load the cloths into the machine I did not feel so good so I sat down. When my mother arrived she asked why I was just sitting and I told her I did not feel well. This is when I started to pass out. Mother was so afraid and did not know what to do she began to cry. I remember her yelling and asking me what was wrong. I could not respond because I was out and had no idea what was going on.

Once I came to, my mother took me home and laid me down, but I still did not feel any better. She said that she was going to take me to the doctor the very next day to see what was wrong. The next day my brother, sister, mother and I got up to start our day, mother dropped my brother and sister off at school and she took me to the doctor. I still do not know the real reason why I would pass out, but I knew that I wanted to be normal and for all of the pain to stop.

The next year we moved again. I often wondered how Mister had the money to do what he did and why we had to move every year. We really did not want to move this year and we all cried. He yelled at us, "Shut up with all of that crying or else!" I wanted to tell my mother so bad, "Would you please speak up and defend us, we are your children not his," but I didn't say anything.

This last move, my mother started to work late nights and would leave us at home with Mister. One day, my brother had done something that Mister did not like and he began to whip my brother with a belt leaving marks on him. My brother cried so badly and I felt sorry for him. My sister and I cried and begged Mister to leave our brother alone, but he kept beating him until my brother broke and ran into his room.

When I was ten years old, we moved again and this house was really nice with four bedrooms, a big backyard, large kitchen, and once again we all had our own room. Our life did a 360 degree shift and we were never stable I mean never. As the parties went on from the night to the early mornings, as a young girl I remember feeling that there are some things children should not be exposed to at an early age. By the time I was ten I had seen and experienced many ungodly things like drugs, nude night clubs, men sleeping with other men and women sleeping with women. Now that I am older I cannot bring myself to partake in things that I was exposed to as a child because I know that it is not in my spirit to do.

All I knew was that I wanted our family back. I wanted to go and live with my grandmother so badly at times, and I often thought I was being selfish and not thinking of the family. I tried my best but I could not bring myself to be happy. We had our own bikes again, a new school and the only thing that was missing in our life was church. You see, when we lived with my step-dad we didn't go to church. Before, we only went to church when my uncle and aunt came by to pick us up every so often. Now, we were lucky if we passed by a church living with this evil man.

Somehow I knew that we would need the Lord in our lives to make it through all of this. We were headed for despair but in it all I knew that my grandmother never stopped praying for us. She loved my mother, sister, brother, and I deeply.

CHAPTER 2
-Fearful, Worried and Abused-

I am eleven years old now what; another year has passed, we are moving again. We turned the corner and there was our home – at least I thought it was. It is so very important for parents to remember whenever they expose their children to things that they are unable to handle. It can result into a negative outcome on that child. Getting back to the move…when we got to the door there was a tall dark lady there to welcome us. Initially, I thought she was the maid, but little did I know she lived there. To go deeper, this was my mother's boyfriend's wife and their two children's home. I cried and screamed, "Take me back! I want my Grandmother! I'm not going to live like this! I asked myself, "How can a mother think that this is the best living environment for us?"

Needless to say the plan went on. That night I cried and cried wanting to go back to live in our old apartment at least we were a family and loved each other. We may not have had all the glitter and glamour but we had each other and we had love.

So now that we are all in, this woman had her two children, one boy and one girl. Just thinking about this makes me appreciate my restoration. My mother exposed us to all the wrong things too soon in life. There were five children, two women and one man. The pathetic adults in this situation shared the same bed. How could one man have so much power over a person to make them live like this and let her small children experience it too? I believe mother knew deep down in her heart it was not right, but she did what he said out of fear. Now, I really hated him. My spirit was wounded and I was really unhappy as a child, always fearful and worried. Unhappy children sometimes grow up and become unhappy adults. The unhappiness would make me act up in school. My mother was at the school many times because of my behavior.

There was always some strange things that went on in our house, I said house because it was not a home not in my heart. I define a home as full of love, clean living, peaceful with one mother, one father, children and a dog. This isn't what we had. I would look at my mother and would ask her, "Why are we living like this?"

She would say to me, "You have too many questions to be so young just accept what is going on and be thankful that your stepdad is providing a nice place for us and we have nice things."

I was always a smart mouth sort of child and had to have the last word. I said I did not like him and that he is not my daddy including that he is tearing our family apart. This man was mean and less than a man to need two women in one house with one bed. I may have been a child but I knew that this was wrong. We were teased at school because my mother and the other woman came to school with us. To make matters worse, the three of them would come on special days and events.

At first my mother stayed home, but then Mister made her get a job working nights and that was when I knew I was really all alone and very scared. This would cause my mother to be away from the house many late nights leaving us at home with Mister. I tried my best not to be scared because mother needed my help most of the time. She always left me in charge to make sure the children had food and that all the clothes were ready for school the next day. We took turns cleaning up the kitchen, we also had to do our homework and leave it for mother to check the next morning before school, which she did.

One day, my stepfather picked us up from school and we stopped by the nude club. My brother, sister and I looked at each other. He then made us get out and go in. I cried wondering what would make a man take children to a nude nightclub to watch women dance. He took my brother in a back room. I really did not know what happened, but the look on my brother's face made me think that something bad happened to him.

I remember that whenever Mister would make us go in the nightclub it was always dark inside. The lights were never on; I guess you could say a dark place is where negative things take place. The club was close to where we lived. One night I was supposed to be in bed but I could not sleep. I went downstairs and saw my stepfather having sex with other men and women. I ran back up to my room and hid under my bed out of fear of what he would do to me because of what I had seen. An hour went by before I heard a door open. I thought it was mother coming home but it was those people leaving. I looked out my bedroom window from the second floor and saw they had on some of the weirdest clothes.

I wished mother was there this way I would know that she was safe. When mother did come home she came up and kissed my brother, sister and I good night. She told us to stay in bed and not come out of our room. The next morning I asked mother why those strange people were in our house and the women and men had their clothes off. I told her, "When you were at work before you came home they were all naked even stepdad." Her reply was, "You were supposed to be in bed."

The next day mother had to work again. My stepfather called for me to come downstairs and get him a glass of water. I said to myself, "He can get his own water," but I went downstairs to give him the water anyway.

As I handed him the water he grabbed me and pulled me toward him, "I have my eyes on you," he told me. This frightened me. I ran back upstairs as fast as I could and told my brother and sister what he said. As I began to cry and tell them, all I could hear was him playing his music and laughing very loudly. We all cried.

I remember one time he was taking a bath and invited me and my sister to take a bath with him. We were children how can this be? My mother was afraid to say anything, because he would beat her.

We shared a bathroom with mother and my stepdad. Their room was on the second floor the only thing that separated our rooms was the hallway leading down the stairs. I closed the door to our bathroom and tried to go to sleep but I could not. I watched my brother and sister fall asleep first and I wrapped them up under the covers this way he could not get to them. I chose to sleep behind the bathroom door locking it from the other side. Some nights I would sleep in my closet to get some rest and hide from that horrible man this way he would not come into my room and pull me out of my bed and force me to have sex with him.

One particular weekend, mother took us to the pool. We had fun because my stepdad was not around. As it began to get dark, we walked back to our townhome. Unfortunately, my stepfather was there and it ruined the whole day. When we got in the house he told me take my towel off so he could see my swim suit. He was smoking his drugs and made me and my mother take a picture in the matching bikini swim suits that he had purchased for us a few days earlier. I told mother that I did not feel comfortable doing this she said it was only a picture so I just stood there while he took the pictures. This man had so much control over our lives, he even had people coming to the house to do our hair so we did not have to go out and get it done.

One day, I recall seeing him kiss another man. I was so scared I thought about the last time he was with those men and women. There were so many things I saw and heard. One night I thought mother was leaving so I walked downstairs only to see mother with another woman. My heart was bleeding with pain and disappointment. He had my mother doing everything and anything.

One night, mother did not come home and I asked my stepfather where was she eventually that morning he told us that mother was in jail. I screamed and yelled at him, "I hate you! I wish you were dead! I wish my mother never have met you, because you have been trouble from day one! You are taking our family down to the gutter."

I could not eat or sleep. The only thing I did was worry and cry about mother. As the evening approached, my stepdad and his wife left. When they returned with mother, my brother, sister and I ran and jumped in mother's arms. She looked so tired and looked bad, but she never talked about what happened. I knew what happened and it did not take long for me to figure it out.

As I began to prepare for the night, all I could think about was the horrible day that mother had been locked up in jail. I could not pull myself together to even think about doing my homework. I guess one could say this along with other things was the reason for me failing my classes. I was always worried and scared. We were children and suffered so much. There was nothing that we could do that would make us safe. I was tormented by my stepfather. I was not able to sleep at night. I lived in fear for me and my mother though I very rarely saw him do anything to my brother and sister. I would ask myself, "Why are mother and I the only ones that are his victims?" Maybe my brother and sister held their abuse and kept it quiet. I do not know but I wanted it to stop. I could not live a happy normal life as kid. I did not know what it was to have fun and do the things that came along with being a young girl.

CHAPTER THREE
-The Night It All Began-

STRANGER IN MY ROOM
I am now entering my teens

I would like to share with you what happened to me when I was a kid
On that day the horrible things that my stepfather came into my room and did
There he stood drunk, naked and not ashamed
Then, after he was finished told me that I was the blame.
I was innocent and a very young child.
Now I have to live with pain rooted deep down inside.
As I laid in my bed sound to sleep,
Every night in my room my stepfather he did creep.
I tried my best to hide all my pain.
But, yet he reminded me that I was the blame.
Who could I tell what happened to me?
My own mother somehow did not believe.
I cried and pleaded for her to listen to what I had to say.
Still she did not believe me so I made plans to run away.
My stepfather would dress nice and where designer suits,
To my surprise he was not a cab driver just a pimp with prostitutes.
You see he had my mother strung out on drugs,
He would take us to watch women dance nude in nightclubs.
Packing guns and alcohol, heroine, and snorting cocaine,
He was making plans for me to do the same.
He would beat my mother and she never fought back,
As a child it was hard to watch my mother be beaten and attacked.

BROKEN CHILD RESTORED WOMAN

I would cry and plead, "Mother, we can just pack up our things and leave."
She would say, "This man loves me, provides for me and gives me what I need."
In her eyes you could see all the pain that she had Being beaten and abused by my stepdad.
Parents, now you have heard what I had to say, Observe, talk and listen to your children each and every day.

One night mother called and said that she and Mister's wife was working late that they would not be home until in the morning. I started to cry and I was really scared. I did all the things that was told of me by mother and helped my brother and sister with whatever they needed. We were all in our bed sound asleep when I felt the covers being taken off of me it was my stepdad, I was very scared. He grabbed me and pulled me towards him, took my night gown off and exposed himself to me. He then started to rub his penis all over my body as I begin to cry harder and shake I did not know whether to scream, fight or call my mother because he was so drunk and he was overpowering me. The more I pulled away from him the more he held me down. I cried, "Please stop, you're hurting me."

He told me to be quiet and not to say anything he reminded me of what he would do to mother. I screamed and I began to fight him off of me but he was much too strong. All I could think about was my baby sister and I did not want him to get to her. He put his hand over my mouth. He was so drunk this night I really had to fight. I broke loose and ran into my room. The next morning I cried as we were all sitting at the table eating breakfast. My mother asked me what was wrong I told her what he had done and she looked at him. She asked him as if I was lying. I cried even more when he said I was lying and mother believed him. He asked mother why would she question him and she said she wanted to know. This must have made him angry because he began to punch and kick mother. He beat her so bad until she started bleeding. I thought about what he said and he made good on his word because I did not let him have his way with me. In my mind, I thought it was my fault that my mother had gotten beaten. I asked mother if we could go back to grandmother's house and she said no this was our house and this is where we would continue to stay.

  The next night he waited until mother and his wife went to work and my brother, sister and his two children were sleep and once again approached me. This time he took me in the room where he, his wife and my mother shared a bed. He showed me nude movies of men and women as he took my clothes off. Initially, I started to cry but remembered that I had to be strong and tough because of what he had done to my mother just a few days before. I decided that whatever he was going to do I was just going to close my eyes and pretend that it was all a bad dream. All I remember is him giving me something very strong to drink and he would always keep a gun close by along with drugs each time. He took his clothes off and took my clothes off, he made me perform oral sex on him and he did the same to me. As I started to cry he told me to shut up and asked me why I was crying. I told him that I was scared and I wanted my mother. He began to smoke his dope and blew some of that smoke in my face again and made me smoke it with him. As I started to feel funny I just laid on the bed crying and crying.

So many times in my life I became bitter and angry at my mother because I told her what was going on and yet she did not believe me and told me I was lying. Even still, I loved and protected her. I also wanted her to leave my step dad. I remember one day I was sick or coming down with a cold. I had a cough and my step dad had given me some cough syrup. After drinking that cough syrup I started feeling really bad and I passed out. As I began to come through all I heard from mother was, "You can stop playing like you are sick. You are not staying home with him."

How could she say something like that to me? I was her child. I was innocent and I did not want what was happening to me to continue to happen. In my heart I believe my mother thought I understood that she was afraid of him and if she said anything to him about this he would beat her again. She had to know all the signs because I was not my normal self. He was asking me to do things for him that was not right. He wanted me to model different clothing. I remember him buying our undergarments and wanting us to model them for him.

One night, as I lay to sleep in my bed, he put his hand over my mouth and pulled me into the bathroom. He told me to put my mouth on his penis and if I did not he would beat my mother. I did not do what he wanted me to do and the next day I got out of school and saw that my mother had a black-eye and a busted lip. I ran to my room and cried feeling this was my fault. From that point on I let him do what he wanted to do to me to keep Mother safe.

One night my stepdad was drunk and he put a chair behind the door so I would not leave. I tried to break free but I could not he turned the music up really loud and I screamed for him to let me out. I would plead with him to let me out but he was too strong and whatever he gave me too drink made me feel funny. I tried to stay awake so that I could leave if he fell asleep. Oh how I wanted to kill him that night; if I could only get to the gun or get to the kitchen to get a knife he would not be able to hurt me or my mother ever again. Needless to say, I cried myself to sleep laying there with no clothes on.

The next morning, mother and his wife came home only to find my step-father and I in the bed without any clothes. I cannot imagine what went through mother's mind finding me like this the next morning with this evil man that she let in to our lives. I tried telling her over and over again what he was doing to me but she did not believe me until she saw with her own eyes. My mother packed our bags and we were going live with our grandmother, but to my surprise we stayed that day.

When mother and my stepdad had fallen to sleep I went into the other room and called my aunt. Crying I told her what he had done to me and made me do the same to him and that he had been beating mother again. Within an hour or two there was a knock on the door, it was my aunt and her husband and he did not play. My cousin who was with them did not play either. They were ready for him. They made us get in the car. I think my uncle had his gun and my stepdad did not say anything. He did not even put up a fight. People say that if a man hits a woman he will not fight another man only because he is less than a man.

⌘ ⌘ ⌘ ⌘ ⌘

I can recall before all this happened one day while my step-father and mother were taking me to school. We were sitting in traffic and I wanted to jump out of the car and scream and plead for help I was in that much pain I just wanted out but fear kept me from it. Imagine fear and pain both at the same time riding down a major street wanting to jump out in the middle of early morning rush hour traffic. I could not breathe, I needed to get out. The very thought of him touching me made my skin crawl, hearing his voice only made it worse. For me, thoughts of killing him crossed my mind many times. I had mixed emotions and I could not tell anyone what I was going through fearing what he would do to Mother.

So I went to school pretending that everything was alright. There were days when I would come home to find my mother with black eyes, busted lips and more from his beatings. I kept telling myself to be strong, that one day she would leave, but to no avail she stayed while the abuse got worse.

Each day would pass and the nights were longer and longer for me. I wanted the mornings to stay forever; it seemed that night was the only time he would come in my room or when mother was at work. I remember mother was not feeling well and wanted to stay home with us, he made her go to work sick. Some day's mother would have to catch a cab or even walk when he did not take her to work.

Mother would work and come home every day. She gave him her earnings and when she did not bring home the money that she should have he would beat her and go through her purse. All we could do was stand and watch. What a hard thing to do? The three of us just hugged each other and cried. Some days we would stay outside longer because we were afraid to go inside where he was. I did not want him to pick me up from school because he would yell and scream. I wished he would just pop a blood vessel and die. I knew this was not the right thing to wish but I wanted him gone and out of our lives so badly. He would then bring other women to our home when mother was not there and have us to wait on them and be nice to them.

One day he picked us up from school only to tell us that mother was in the hospital. I was hurting so badly that I started to scream uncontrollably. This woman, his wife was with him and I asked her what happened and she said they had a big fight. I knew what he had done. I got home and called my grandmother and Aunt when he left the house. I told them that mother was in the hospital and asked if someone would pick us up. He walked in as I hung up the phone and asked me who I was talking to. I told him I called my grandmother and aunt and that they would be picking us up.

He said, "No one is coming to my house and taking you nowhere." I started to cry and my brother and sister were scared and crying too. They were the quiet ones but I was always aggressive and strong. My stepfather would tell me, "You have a lot of mouth to be so young. I know what I need to do for that."

He instructed my sister and brother to go into their rooms. He took his belt off and tried to beat me but I caught the belt and held on to it. He told me to let go of the belt and I told him no and that I was not afraid of him and I fought him with everything I had in me. I let him know that I was not my mother and I would not just stand back and let him beat me. He called me all sorts of names and threatened to kill me. I told him to go right ahead but I would continue to fight with everything I had, that I wasn't afraid and I would never be for him.

In beating my mother he had knocked her teeth out of her mouth, burned her body with cigarettes, and blackened her eyes. When my mother tried to walk he had beat her so hard she could barely move. I cried and I looked my stepdad in his eyes and I told him to take one good look at mother because that would be the last time that he would ever have her in that condition.

Once my mother was released from the hospital and returned home, I guess she had enough. She called my uncle and her sister they came and got us again and we left. In my heart I knew once mother had gotten better she would go back. I had this feeling deep inside of me that one day he will hit mother and her life would be ended and my brother, sister, and I would not have our mother anymore. Within a few weeks mother was making plans to go back to my stepfather and once again we all moved back with the horrible man.

CHAPTER FOUR
-Running Away to Be Safe-

The abuse continued. I thought to myself, "Now that I am going to high school maybe the abuse will stop." But never the less, it continued and I was still afraid. I can say that while at school I felt safe. I was on the girls' softball team and this helped me to channel my negative energy and put it all in the softball team at school. I started doing very well in my class work. I had a best friend at school that I was able to talk to about what was going on at my home and she suggested that I go to the principal and let her know, I decided not to.

1978- This year the movie, "The Wiz," had come out and I remember mother, brother, sister and I went to the movies. After the movie we went shopping in one of the biggest shopping malls in Houston. We browsed through many of the stores in the Galleria. Spending time with mother without stepdad made me happy. We had a wonderful time; we went ice skating and laughed at each other falling on the ice. This was a family fun day. The next week we went to see the movie, "Grease." At this point, the abuse had stopped and there weren't any more fights between my stepdad and mother. I thought how cool it was for us to go to the movies then shopping being so young. I thought things were changing.

We went to dinner just mother, sister, brother and I. We laughed, acted like children being silly, and mother laughed along with us. When we returned home there was my step dad sitting in his chair. He asked mother where she had been, she told him she had taken off from work to spend time with us. This made him very angry. He started pushing mother and slapping her. I told him, "Wait, stop do not do that to her!" My brother and sister stood frozen with fear.

I told him if he hit her again I would call the police and he would be arrested. Now that I was old enough to take the steps to take, he really did not want to challenge me. For once, I thought I had the upper hand and he was scared of me. Little did I know, the next day he had mother all alone and took advantage of her. I had to remind myself not to say or do anything that would put her in danger if I was not around to defend her.

I remember my stepdad coming home with milk shake products and selling them. He held meetings at our home and tried to get others to invest. He even invited some of my mother's family members and a few of them attended. As he sold more and more of the products the house became saturated with even more people. Eventually, we were told to get dressed and sit, watch and listen. We had to sit and watch for hours at a time.

One weekend there was this big party and everyone was there with nowhere to sit. Mother made plenty of food and there was a lot of liquor and some drugs too. Not wanting us to see what was going on, mother made us go upstairs and stay in our room.

One night mother had gone to work and my stepdad was back to his old ways again. He would get high, drunk and fall in the middle of the floor and that is where mother would find him. It was football night over our house and my stepdad's children were at the house. It was the year of the Houston Oilers and we thought they were headed for the Super Bowl.

It did not happen but the City of Houston put on a big welcome home event for them. My step-father was using drugs, drinking, and there that gun was again. While watching the game the gun was laying on the table and my stepdad's daughter picked up the gun. I took it from her and before I knew it my stepdad took the gun away and told us that we should never play with a loaded gun. I asked myself why he would leave a loaded gun around children.

 When I lived with my grandmother before moving back with my mother, grandmother signed us up for piano lessons and I met a boy. When I moved back with mother we continued to stay in touch. I told mother about him and that I liked him. She asked me his name. I told her. I asked if he could come and visit me sometimes and she said she would have to meet his parents. I told her that he lived with his mother and that his father did not live with him. I guess my stepfather did not like this and he made sure I did not talk to him that often.

 There were months that passed and I had not spoken with my boyfriend. One weekend mother said that she had a surprise for me and that we were going for a ride, what I did not know was my stepdad would come along with us. As we headed in the direction where my grandmother lived I was happy because I thought we were going to see grandmother, but we did not. Mother went to pick up my boyfriend and brought him out to the house. When we all arrived my mother told me that the two of us could go to the pool. My boyfriend and I hung out by the pool with my brother and sister and had lots of fun. Mother fixed us dinner and we all ate, watched TV and talked. I thought how nice it would have been if my stepdad was not there. My boyfriend asked me when we were talking if I was alright, because he noticed that I would become uneasy when my stepdad would get close to me or walk past me. I told him no and I began to cry and told him what he had done to me. He told my mother that he wanted to go home. This is when we all got in the car and took him to his house. Later on that night he called me and asked me if I was okay. He said that he was going to tell his mother what my stepdad was doing to me. We talked on the phone for many hours. I felt safe with him and knowing that someone believed me finally made it a little easier to bare. I was now planning my day to run away and never come back. I made up in my mind that if mother wanted to stay she could but I was leaving and I was leaving soon.

Mother told me that I needed to stop spending so much time talking on the phone with my boyfriend. I told her okay. One evening, my stepdad had come home from work and mother was at work. I had just finished eating dinner with my brother and sister. They went upstairs to take their baths, I stayed down to clean the kitchen, and once again my stepdad smoked his dope in front of me. He did not care. I was so afraid that I called my mother and asked her if I could call my boyfriend and talk to him. She told me I had to ask my stepdad and I said, "Why? You are my mother."

She told me just do what she said to keep the peace. I did just that with no more questions asked while mother was at work. On this particular night, my stepfather was drunk out of his mind and he took me downstairs and made me drink that cough syrup once again. He told me that he wanted me to dance for him again. I told him I wanted my mother and please leave me alone and that I had a boyfriend. All he did was laugh and told me to do what he said or he would beat mother and put her back in the hospital. I started to cry and told him no and I was not going to do it, "Okay," he said. "The next time you see your mother she will be in a hospital bed."

"Oh Lord, help me," I prayed. "Get me out of this house, it's starting back again, I'm scared! I just want to be free from all of this."

The next morning I got to school and went to the principal's office to use the phone and called my boyfriend to let him know what he did to me. He told me that he would come and get me. I told him I was not going to leave without my brother and my sister and he said that they could come too. When I got home from school mother was not there and I became very afraid. All I could think was that my mother was in the hospital beaten and hurt, but she was at work.

Later that night, I had to fight for my life and defend my mother. I recall my stepfather beating my mother so badly. Hearing her scream hurt me deeply but I could not do anything because she always told me not to interfere because he would kill me. Somehow I had convinced myself I would rather die than to sit, listen and watch my mother being beaten the way he beat her. This particular year I was on the girls' baseball team and I brought my baseball bat home. My brother, sister and I sat on the edge of our bed crying while mother screamed and cried from the beating by our stepfather.

"I'm going in there," I told my brother and sister, and they asked me not to because he would hurt me. "I don't care," I told them before kicking the door in. I looked at my step-father and told him, "if you hit mother again, I'll take this bat and knock your head off!"

As he approached me and began to punch me in my face I shocked him by fighting back – I wasn't like mother. This must had frightened him because he left. I went to console mother. The both of us were crying when I asked her, "Mother, why do you stay?" Her reply was, "I love him." How on earth can you love someone that treats you so unkind and beats you, how can you love a person like this? Her reply was, "I do not know."

I cleaned mother up, washed her face and put her to bed. As I lay in mother's arms she said, "I wish I had your strength and courage." I told her, "You do, all you have to do is walk away and never look back just leave him." I held my mother and we talked until she fell asleep. I did not bother going into my room to go to bed I just laid there. I wanted mother to be safe and to watch over her.

This night homework was not important once again and I did not care about it. Each time I heard a car pass I would ease away and look out of the window making sure that it was not my stepfather coming back. As the night went on I saw daybreak not having any sleep because I had been up all night. I wanted to stay at home with mother but she made me go to school. I went into my room where my brother and sister were and I suggested that one of us learn how to drive so that the next time he beat mother we would take the car and leave once he fell asleep.

I went to school without doing my homework. My teacher asked why my homework wasn't completed, but I did not say a word. I took the bad grade and that was that. You see, when you are unhappy at home it has a great impact on everything that you do turning just about everything negative around you. It was almost the weekend and I could not wait because mother would take us to see our grandmother for a few hours. That time he was gone for two weeks.

One Thursday night before the weekend, my stepfather had come home drunk. He told us to have our chores done and he would be back. He had to pick mother up from work. I had cooked dinner and waited but still did not hear or receive a phone call from mother. I fed my sister and brother told them to take their baths and they went to bed. I waited and waited for mother. I looked out of the window and my stepfather's car was parked across the street I said to myself, "That is strange, why would he park his car across the street?"

By then I knew it was bad news. I sat on the stairs. There was a turn of the key at the front door. The door opened and I ran to the door, when it opened it was mother. I was so glad to see her and to make sure she was alright because of the night before. In walked mother and behind her was my stepfather. Mother and my stepfather sat at the table on this night he told me to sit with them. This was so unusual I just did what I was told because I did not want him to do anything to mother.

Comfort words – it is funny how we learn to protect at such an early age not being aware of what and really the real reason why. Comfort is to bring healing.

> Com·fort·ed, com·fort·ing, com·forts. 1. To soothe in time of affliction or distress. 2. To ease physically; relieve. n. a state of physical ease and freedom from pain or constraint, consolation for grief or anxiety.

All of these things are what I was going through trying to make sure that my mother and I was safe. When one finds themselves in a physical state of discomfort, we must rely on the inner strength that our Creator has given to us. I do believe that the Lord gave me all of my inner strength in my young life to be a comfort for my mother.

That night the three of us sat at the table. At first we just sat quietly, no one said anything. Mother had fear in her eyes as my stepfather began to speak. He was very dramatic, vocal and loud. He placed drugs, his keys, and a gun on the table. He told me, "You know I do not like the way that you have been keeping this house, it's never clean and my dinner is always late, and you always make me feel uncomfortable in my own home."

Whenever I would try to speak he would tell me to shut up. I told him, I can say what I very well please! What you're saying isn't true. He replied, "Why were you up peeping out of the window when you are supposed to be in bed?" I told him I was looking for mother and wanted to make sure that she made it home safe."

This is when he began to call me out of my name. I said, mother, are you going to just sit there and let him talk to me like this?

She said nothing. The only word that was written on her face was fear. He told me this night that I would not be going to school anymore and that I was going to work for him in the night club dancing. I said, "your prostitute dancing nude and to make you money? Oh no, I will not." I told him that he was a liar I had dreams but all he did was laugh. "Dreams? You cannot even make passing grades you do not have any dreams."

He told me that I was failing out of school, my grades were poor and in life I was not going to be anything. I told him it was because of all of the abuse and the beatings that I witnessed in this house. I got up and started leaving the room when he pushed me back into the chair and told me that I was going to stay up all night and listen to his plans. He slapped me in my face and told me to take some drugs. When I refused, he picked up the gun and placed it to my head and told me if I did not take the drugs that he would kill me in front of mother. I looked at mother as she started to cry and beg me to take the drugs.

"You may as well kill me," I told him. "Each time you hit mother and make me listen and witness, little pieces of my life leaves me each time. So pull the trigger and do us all a favor. I will be dead, you will be in jail and mother will never be the same ever in her life." To my surprise, he laid the gun down and started to use drugs. He made mother use them with him. I cried and cried.

The both of them were stoned out of their minds when he hit me. As I tried to fight back, mother jumped in on his side. I broke free, ran to the phone and dialed 9-1-1 and the police came. When they got there I pleaded with the police, "please, please take me I do not want to be here I want to go and live with my grandmother."

Mother told the police that I had done something bad at school and they were correcting me for it. My heart felt pain like never before. I still loved and worried about mother that night ever so greatly and I cried and cried still not getting any sleep. I stayed and didn't leave.

When they had finally fallen asleep I went upstairs with my brother and sister and saw that they were crying. I could see in their eyes that they were afraid I told them I was going to run away. It was so bad I wanted to jump out of the second story window in my bedroom of our town home. My brother and sister asked me not to say that I would hurt myself. At this point I really did not care. I said to myself, "I am already hurting, what could be worse than what I am going through?"

The next morning my mother and stepfather took us to school. I had already made plans to run away the moment they dropped me off at school. I thought about what would happen to mother, brother and sister if I ran away. All I could do was pray for their safety as well as my own. I continued to think of ways to run away so that I could be safe. The next night my mother went to work and left us home with my stepfather.

While making my plans to run away I thought long and hard about my mother, sister and brother. It was night time and I thought I was the only one awake when mother came into our room and said she had some bad news. She told us that our uncle had died. All I could do was scream and cry uncontrollably. My sister, brother and I could not stop crying. I thought about my cousins and how they must have felt losing their father. I remember one year he played Santa Claus. He was like a father to us all.

We went to the service to be supportive to my aunt and her children it was such a sad service we all cried. My stepfather did not attend because our family did not care for him at all. When we got back to our house he had all kinds of gifts waiting for us. When we settled down and things tried to go back to normal, I knew it was time to leave. I thought to myself, what if it was my grandmother that had died? I would have been forced to live in that abusive house and my stepfather wishes of me being a nude dancer would have come true." From then on I prayed and asked God to keep us safe and let my grandmother live for a very long time.

As I prepared for school the next morning all I could think of was that I was going to be with my grandmother. My stepdad dropped me off at school and I went into the school building as if I was going to school. When he drove off I walked to the pay phone and called my grandmother to let her know that I was on my way I was just waiting on the bus. I waited and waited on the bus it took forever. Once the bus arrived I prayed that my stepfather was not somewhere watching me. I got on the bus, knelt down on the floor and I started crying. The bus driver asked me what was wrong. "Please, Mr. Bus Driver, just drive," I said,

He begins to drive and I cried and shook until we got out of the area where I lived. Once out of the area I began to feel better. I asked him to take me to my grandmother's house on the Southeast side of town off of Cullen. The closer I got to my grandmother's house I started to cry more and more longing to see my grandmother's face and to feel her arms around me. The bus turned the corner and I saw my grandmother's street, "Oh my, God, there is the house!"

"Thank you so much, Mr. Bus Driver, thank you, thank you." He opened the doors of the bus and I could see my grandmother standing in the front of the house. I ran towards her and she ran to meet me. Though it was a short distance it seemed to last forever as I anticipated her embrace.

"You are here, baby, you made it!" My grandmother said to me. I sobbed uncontrollably and she told me she was thankful to God that I was safe now and that now everything would be alright.

CHAPTER FIVE
-16 Pregnant and Married

    Now that I am living with my grandmother, I feel safe and not so afraid. Later on that year my brother and sister moved with my grandmother. I'm at a new school making new friends and active in different activities in my school. Mother would come and see us from time to time; each time I would beg and plead with her not to go back but she always went back.

    Grandmother would let us go visit mother every so often because this was mother's wish and she knew that if she wanted us that she could get us at any time. It was hard but I did. At first, I spent a lot of time out there which really concerned my grandmother and she stopped this right away. One day as I lay in my bed I overheard my grandmother, aunts, and uncle discussing getting full custody of us so that mother could not take us back into that environment. We would never go see mother again. After that, I spent a lot of my time thinking about how hard it was for her not having us around. Each time mother would come around she looked so bad. She had lost a lot of weight and this broke grandmother's heart seeing mother like this but grandmother continued to pray. There had been many times I would find grandmother asleep in her favorite chair, her Bible in her lap and a small picture of mother on the page that she was reading. Somehow, I knew she never stopped praying for mother.

    A year has passed and I began to date this guy my grandmother did not approve of. Somehow, my uncle convinced her that I was a teenager and I should have a boyfriend.

One day he and his mother came over to the house to meet my grandmother. The women talked and we sat right there making sure nothing went on between us, but my grandmother told me that she really did not care for him at all. I guess one would say, "Grandmother knew best." The next year passed and I found myself rebelling and acting out because I had fallen in love with his guy. My grandmother saw my grades declining and my behavior in school was growing worse. I started to hang out with the wrong group of girls and started skipping school. Lying one bad lie and doing one bad thing leads to another thing that was not allowed in my grandmother's house. I guess my stepfather's words were beginning to surface into my life. The sad part was I was not living in the same house with him and my past had followed me although I had ran away to be safe.

My boyfriend and I would skip school and I would go over to his house while his mother was at work. I said to myself, "everyone is doing it, so it won't hurt just this one time."

One time led to many and this is where I made the mistake of looking at what others were doing and not being a leader of my own actions. As we spent more time together and skipped school, one day he wanted to have sex with me. I was totally against it because I was still trying to forget the sexual abuse that I had endured by my stepfather. When my boyfriend would kiss me I would pull back and tell him, "No." He told me that I should forget what happened, that he was not my stepfather. I told him that I was not ready and we should wait because we were too young to have sex. He said he loved me and if I loved him I would do it. I told him I was not ready.

    My grandmother gave me chances to clean up my act and get back on the right path with my school but I continued to do the opposite. The next year my grandmother took me out of all the activities. I was only permitted to go to school, church, and back home. This angered me and pushed me closer and closer to my boyfriend, we started to have sex every time we would see each other.

    My grandmother house was a three-bedroom home for her, and the three of us to live in because we had been through so much. This was the family home for all of her children and grandchildren to come to have family gatherings. One thing my grandmother had was a whole lot of love and made sure that we stayed close as a family. We had family gatherings every week if not every day. Grandmother told us how important family was and she demanded that we love and respect each other all of the time. Most importantly, she stressed that we place the Lord first in our lives. She gave us all she had and could give. My mother's sister helped with the home furnishings and we had our own rooms. In regards to my aunts, when they would come over it was family time and it always felt like Christmas. Even with my grandmother and all the family around, to me, there was still something missing, my dear mother.

    On this particular night the telephone rang and my grandmother answered the phone it was my mother she was screaming in the background, "Mother, please help me he's going to kill me!" My grandmother dropped the phone and begins to cry, my aunt asked my grandmother, "Mother, what's wrong?" All she did was continued to cry and said, "he is going to kill my baby." My aunt asked "who?"

"It's Emma, he's beating her and now he is making me listen," my grandmother said. This is when my aunt picked up the phone and heard mother pleading for her life. Mother was screaming and screaming she could barely get a word in. My Aunt pleaded with mother again, but still nothing until my stepdad got on the phone. He told my aunt that when he gets through beating her she will wish that she was dead and that he would kill her.

My aunt was a very strong honorable woman but when she spoke you better believe that everyone listened and did what she said. She told my stepdad if he ever put his finger in the phone to dial my grandmother's number and let her hear him beat mother that they would not be able to identify his face or body when she got through with him. I just got up and ran into my room and cried fearing the worse in the back of my mind. I knew one day the phone would ring and it would be very bad news about mother.

Now that I am older I wonder why mother stayed and allowed him to abuse her for all of those years. It is sad for someone to say that they love and care for you and beat you the way that my stepdad beat my mother. Unfortunately, not only did he beat her but had her doing things that were ungodly.

If I may go into the mind of my mother while raising her children...she probably thought she would raise us without all the abuse, the guilt, hurt and shame. My mother raised us the best way that she knew how and gave us all she had. One thing I know is that my mother loved us. It was just she had someone that had a much stronger hold on her and did not know how to get out of the abusive relationship. She was scared of what he would do to her, bound by fear, substance abuse and longing for love. Unfortunately, she sought it in a man that abused her for years and eventually caused her to die at an early age.

The phone call ruined our family get together but we still remained strong, hopeful, and prayerful that mother would be safe in an unsafe environment; and one day she would have the courage to leave. My grandmother laid a strong foundation in our home that no matter what we went through, no matter how bad it looked, that we must remain strong in our faith. She demanded that we pray about everything that was evil and not of God, always saying that we can make it through prayer. I did not understand what she really was saying and why they did not go and get mother. I did not understand why they would all be silent holding hands and pray or how family night was able to continue after that.

As I grew older grandmother would sit me down and tell me, "Baby, when you have bad things to happen and there's not a whole lot that you can do, you must turn it over to the Lord and leave it there knowing that He will fix it."

That evening after everyone left I stayed up and made sure that the house was clean and had more talks with grandmother. I wanted to have faith like she did because what mother was going through I wanted to be able to pray and have faith to make sure when I did see mother again I would be able to tell her what grandmother told me.

My grandmother raised her children, grandchildren, great grandchild, and great-great grandchildren and ran her own day care. She worked hard in different organizations in the church. She was the church mother, grandmother, sister, aunt, leader of many groups within our family and the church. Most of our family went to my grandmother's church. If they did not go they may as well have been members because they were always there helping and supporting grandmother with everything. This is why I wanted to stay up and listen to her because she was full of wisdom and had a loving and caring spirit. She was a joy to be around no matter what she was facing in her own personal life. My grandmother would put herself last and others first. I remember while raising us she gave and sacrificed many nights. It was hard on her sometimes. When we did not have food to eat my grandmother would have a cup of coffee, a slice of toast, smoke her cigar and read her Bible until she fell to sleep.

As a child staying with my mother was really hard for me because of all the things that I saw and went through. I always felt that she was a good mother very loving and caring, but she just had a stronghold that had her bound in so many different ways. One day we got a phone call from the hospital letting us know that mother had tried to kill herself again. She had also been beaten very badly and her leg had been broken. My aunt went to the hospital and picked up my mother and brought her home to grandmother's house. We were very glad that mother was with us safe.

As mother healed and got stronger we all began to have fun times again as a family. One day mother told me that I had an older sister that my father had by a previous relation with another woman. I told her I wanted to meet my sister and we got in the car and went over to where my sister and her mother lived. We talked for hours and shared our life stories and exchanged numbers to keep in touch. I remember the same year my older sister that was nineteen was planning her wedding. She asked me to be a hostess and I was really happy. We all went to the wedding and had a great time.

    A few weeks passed and one day after school, my grandmother looked so sad. I ran into my room and I called mother, this is when grandmother told me that she had gone back to my stepdad. My heart dropped. Weeks later my grades dropped and I was kicked out of school. I had skipped school on a particular day and gone over to my boyfriend's house. We were all drinking and having sex. I was happy and mad all at the same time wondering if my mother was okay, missing my mother, and praying that things would get better. At sixteen I was out of control.

    When I returned to school I got into a fight and the principal called my mother because this was the number I changed when I worked in the principal's office. I knew that the number was disconnected but to my surprise they had reconnected the phone. My mother answered and she and my stepdad came and picked me up. This was not good because I did this to myself not being obedient to my grandmother. How did I end up back in a place where I was abused, scared, worried and in pain? And to make matters worse, my boyfriend told me that he had enlisted in the army. I told mother although I was back with her I still wanted to be with and missed grandmother dearly. She told me it was my choice that I could stay with her or go back, but I would not be able to return if I decided to go with my grandmother. This was hard for me to accept but as we made plans for me to go back I continued to stay with my grandmother.

I realized that I had not gotten my period for two months. I called my older sister and told her. She went to the clinic with me. We both took a pregnancy test she thought she was pregnant given she had just gotten married. Consequently, I was the one with child. I started to cry and she asked me what I wanted to do. I told her I did not know and that I would ask my boyfriend when he returned from the army in a month. This was my senior year in high school and I had to go to Kay On-going Education center, a school for unwed mothers.

When he came back his mother and I met him at the airport. I told him that I was pregnant and he was very excited and wanted me to marry him because he would be leaving for a year to go overseas. I said, "yes," because I could not go back to my stepfather's house and wanted a better life for my baby. I did not want my stepfather around my baby and I wanted a family. I thought this would make a better life than the one that I had experienced. We made plans for the wedding and things were a disaster. Mother was still getting beat by my stepdad, no one wanted me to marry my boyfriend, no one wanted to be in the wedding, but we continued to make plans. My grandmother told me to just have the baby and not marry him because he was going to ruin my life.

As we prepared for the wedding I had one last night at my stepfather's house. It was morning and mother had left me asleep and gone to the store. I woke up and my stepfather was standing over me and for some reason I was not afraid. I got up and looked him in the face and told him, "whatever you are thinking about doing, remember my whole family has their eyes on you now! I told all my mother's sisters what you did to me."

He stood back and looked at me and shook his head, by this time my sister had come to the house, it was the day of my wedding December 22, the year 1979.

Now that I was going to be a mother I would have to take care of my own child. I remember thinking back that this would be a cake walk for me because I had taken care of my own brother and sister, but little did I know that it was not that easy, but having my mother, grandmother and my mother in-law really helped. My grandmother said that she was not going to attend the wedding because she did not approve. She felt that I would have to live my mother's life all over again. I told her that she was wrong, but she saw something that I could not see. On the day of the wedding, I said if grandmother was not coming I was not going to walk down the aisle.
One hour passed no grandmother, two hours passed no grandmother, finally they said I would have to make a decision and I was getting ready to call the wedding off, but in walked grandmother. She came to me and said, "Baby, I'm here only because I love you, but I do not approve of this at all."

The wedding was supposed to begin at one o'clock but I did not walk down the aisle until almost three o'clock. We were married and went to the reception; all of my classmates were there. We had a lot of fun that night, but I wanted mother to come with us. Everyone was leaving, my new husband and I went to our hotel and we were settled in, then there was a knock on the door it was my stepdad and my mother. He was really drunk and I guess because he paid for the wedding he said he was staying with us. How sad I was. My mother and I sat up all night while he and my husband went downstairs. It wasn't until early morning they came back up they decided to leave and I was glad.

When we got to my mother in-law's house she was happy but sad because she told me that they had gotten a phone call saying my mother was in the hospital and that he had thrown her out of the car on the freeway. She had been beaten, stabbed and had cigarette burns all over her body. I cried when my mother-in-law told me. She told me to calm down and to think of my baby.

Looking back on those horrible days reminds me of how I wanted to give up many times. I had dreams in my heart, I wanted to go to college, get a good job and take care of my mother so that she would not have to work another day in her life. Well, of course this did not happen. I found myself with a newborn baby on the way and still worried about my mother.

BARBARA HILL-JACKSON

"Trusting God in Singlehood"
By Barbara Jackson

While waiting patiently for the man that God has for me,
Being single isn't as bad as it seems to be.
For you see, when I fix my heart on the things for the Lord
I know that I will receive a better reward.

As I reflect back over my life I once used to be someone's wife,
You see my house was no longer a home,
Because, one day my husband decided to roam.

As time went on I became a single parent,
I prayed to the Lord that all my burdens he would carry
My house was filled with great pain, but I trusted in the Lord
so I did not complain.

For you see being single with three children to feed,
I knew that the Lord would supply all my needs.
I always worked hard and kept a job,
My grandmother raised me to put all my faith and trust in
God.

No matter what the test as a single mother I did my best,
I made many mistakes along the way, oh how I thank God for
his saving grace.
When I became single and all alone I kept on praying to God
to make my house again a happy home.
A place to raise my children where they would be safe every day,
walking by faith.

When I would make mistakes throughout the years I would cry
and shed many tears

BROKEN CHILD RESTORED WOMAN

But through it all in my life now that I'm single and no one's wife everything turned out allright.
Being single is not so bad; because you cannot miss the love that beat and kept you so sad.
I rather be single the rest of my life, than to be an abused and neglected wife.
I raised my children and gave them all I had, with no help from their dead beat dad.

Now that the children are all grown, I'm still single but very strong.
I ask myself why my life isn't filled with turmoil and desperation,
I found a new church home where visions of blessing, enrichment and empowering words being taught
in a City located in Rosharon at "The Word of Restoration."

CHAPTER SIX
-Repeating the Cycle with Hidden Fears-

You have read my story and now understand how I was exposed to too much at a young age, the reason I ran away, got pregnant and why I got married at the age of 16. I started repeating the cycle of what I had lived for many years of my life.

I found myself about to have a nervous breakdown when I recognized that my own marriage was repeating the cycle of what I had lived in as a child. I had convinced myself that I would never be my mother and let a man beat and abuse me, but it happened. I did not learn until my late thirties about breaking generational curses until I read the Word of God. I wish I had this many years ago. This was all new to me.

When I compare my life to all the things that I was exposed to, to what I had been taught. What a wonderful transformation? Being married and having a child was easy for me, but the hard part was being abused and letting my own daughter witness the very same thing that I had seen my mother go through. All I had to do was close my eyes and see my mother and myself as a little girl, then I would open my eyes and it was happening in my own life. I was a woman with a child to care for, I knew I had to make the right decision for her but I did not know why I chose the same abusive life to raise my precious daughter.

She was a beautiful funny kind of baby and everyone loved her, but what they did not know was that this funny little baby girl had to live in fear, worry and abuse. She was abused at times herself, but I spoke up and I fought back, but wait, this is my childhood life all over again. What a sad thing to go through and then take your very own child through the same thing.

Mothers, listen, I know they say love is blind, but love should not be so blind that it puts our children at risk and does not give them a chance to experience a home filled with love and happiness without the presence of abuse. I recall one time I was beaten so badly I was sitting on my bed and my three-year daughter old wiped my tears and told me, "Momma, it is going to be okay we can go live with grandmother."

Are you seeing the same picture? I lived in an abusive home wanting to go with my grandmother and helping my mother after she was beaten. Now my baby was telling me the same thing, "we can go live with grandmother," after seeing me abused. Repeating the cycle – it was so easy to leave but why was it so hard to stay away? Because, this is what I had seen my mother do in my childhood years. I had learned what I lived and I did just that. Each time I would go back the beatings got worse until he charged my baby and this is something that a mother will not just sit back and let anyone do. So when I did leave I stayed gone for a year until he convinced me that he would go to counseling so I agreed to make it work one last time. However, this time when I went back, I had gotten pregnant. Why? I asked myself, but I found myself getting ready to be a mother for the second time. So I said to myself, "I better get my life together, if he hits me again I am leaving and never returning."

The year was 1984 and I was eight months pregnant. I was at my home and had fallen asleep. I heard a voice saying, "Barbara, child come home," it was my grandmother's voice. She lived in another city but it was like she was in the same room with me. Little did I know my husband had purchased a gun and was thinking about killing himself? The one thing I know is if you are thinking about killing yourself, then you will think about killing those around you when you are hurting like he was because he knew I was leaving him. On this particular night, my husband had come home mad and drunk and I feared for my life. He beat me until I went into premature labor.

Needless to say, my baby almost died that night. They put my baby on a ventilation machine. It was hard but he made it through. I ended up leaving my husband and my mother took the kids back to the other city to care for until I was able to get on my feet to provide for them. I would fly from Dallas to Houston to see the children. I remember staying in Dallas hoping that I could find work but my husband wanted me to stay with him. The children were with my parents and his parents which made things a lot easier. Years passed and we both agreed to go our separate ways. I had come home to visit my mother and family in the year of 1987 when mother told me that she had been to the doctor and they found cancer in her breast and it had to be removed.

I had never seen mother so sad even when she was with my stepdad she would wear a smile but this news made her very sad. I told her that it would be okay but they had to remove her breast and the next year the report showed that the Cancer had spread. The doctors wanted to talk to us. Mother looked me in my eyes and said she did not want to die and I told her she would not. I went back to Dallas to prepare my final move to take care of my mother. I prepared to head back to Houston the next morning when I had gotten a phone call that night from my brother saying I should hurry home because mother had grown very ill.

My neighbor offered to take me to Houston, so the next morning I packed up the kids and we started on our trip. It was a bright clear day, no rain in the forecast. We were halfway through our trip, about six o'clock, when it began to rain. It poured so bad that we had to pull on the side of the road. After the rain stopped we proceeded to drive on into Houston. I remember arriving at the hospital and the head nurse wanted to talk to me. I told her I would speak with her once I saw mother. Another nurse looked at me and asked if I was pregnant I told her yes. She said, "I'm sorry but your mother expired at six o'clock this evening."

I passed out. I could hear my children screaming and I tried to come through but I could not, "Lord, please help me, help."

They started slapping me on my face and putting a cold towel on my face to bring me through. The situation took me back to the time I had found my own mother lying on the floor near death. I had to witness her just lying there and now my children seeing the same thing, "repeating the cycle." The Lord had a better plan and when I came through it all I wanted to see my grandmother. I felt like it was my stepfather's fault that he had taken my mother away from me. At this time my step father had remarried and still lived in the Houston area.

How can I go on? What am I supposed to do without her in my life? I just wanted to wake up and this all be a bad dream but it was not. I could not remember how to get to my grandmother's house I was so destroyed by the news of mother dying, my aunt had to come and get me and my babies from the hospital. My mother may be gone but never will I forget all of the sacrifices, the hardship, the beatings, and all she endured. She was strong in her own way; even when at times we may have thought that she was weak and frail. The strength she had was in her own courage to face all odds and strength to help her stay in a bad relationship even when she could not pull herself to leave.

There are a lot of Emma's out there like my mother that want to leave but just do not know how and cannot find the strength to leave. We must be their strength and help them find the will that God has for their life. Mother had a man that beat her and broke the very essence of spirit, but he could not touch her soul. She had a sweet loving and caring soul that only belongs to God. She endured many beatings and would not leave. He had her strung out on all sorts of drugs, doing things that lowered her self-worth but she still endured. She went through chemo and radiation for the Breast Cancer and when the Lord saw all of the pain and suffering she had to endure he welcomed her to a place where she would dwell in safety for the rest of her life.

"Sleep well my loving mother," I wrote this poem for you and all those that have lost their battle to Breast Cancer. This poem is also dedicated to all of the Breast Cancer survivors as well and to those that are battling Breast Cancer.

BROKEN CHILD RESTORED WOMAN

Writing for the Cure

So I hear you have been to your doctor and they have ran a few tests,
Now the report shows that they may have to cut off one or both of your breasts.

Do not be discouraged about what you're going through,
The Lord sees everything and He will take care of you.

Whether it is chemo or radiation therapy just cast your cares on
The Lord and do not let them worry you.
You may even lose some or all of your hair do not be dismayed
Jesus will always be there

Some treatments are different in everyone but you must believe that your
"VICTORY" has already been won.
It really doesn't matter the level of your decease The Lord Jesus Christ has borne your infirmities

You may have lost a family member or a friend just know that they fought
The good fight of faith until the very end.
You may even be going through this struggle yourself
Keep the faith in Jesus because he is your help.

Don't you know you are stronger than anything you may face
There are others supporting you and running for the race

We will pray and stand hand-n-hand that's for sure
We won't give up until they have found a cure

BARBARA HILL-JACKSON

You will find love and support in the Susan G. Komen Foundation
Helping women all over the country and in every nation

Written by: Barbara Jackson
10/15/2012
Dedicated to my mother, Emma K. Robinson. Gone too soon but not forgotten May 22, 1988.
Dedicated to my aunt, Mrs. Patricia Porter, who is a survivor 32 years.
Dedicated to each and every woman standing hand-in-hand.

Now that my mother had gone home to be with the Lord my heart was very sad. In 1988, I found myself pregnant with two children, no job, no home and grieving the loss of my mother. As we began to prepare for mother's home going services I returned back to that frightened little girl wondering about tomorrow and finding a place to live for me and my small child and preparing for the baby that I was carrying. I could not provide for my children all I could think of was mother not with me anymore I just wanted to die and to make matters worse I had to go back to mother's house all alone with my babies. I did not have a car and everything was so overwhelming. All I could think of was killing myself to escaping living. I was thinking of my losses and not what I had to live for.

This is what happens many times in a person's life when adversity, hardship, and difficulties arise. When we suffer a great loss we want out and want the pain to stop. It is so assuring when you have a close praying family and friends that will intercede and be there on your behalf to help you through the hard times. My family began to work on helping me find a nice place for my children and I to live. After a while the pain subsided but I still had depressed moments in my life after losing mother and not getting a chance to see her and say, "good-bye." Being able to tell her that I loved her would have made it easier for me to deal with her passing. I would say to myself over and over again, "Mother, I love you and I am sorry that I did not move back home sooner."

After my baby was born I named her after my mother. The same year, things had begun to look a little better for me. I started to work so that I could support my children and help my grandmother with the house. One year passed and I still had bouts of depression. I had a panic attack while driving one day and could not breathe; I felt like I was choking and needed air. I pulled over on the side of the road to compose myself but each time I tried to drive I felt as if I was going to pass out. I sat there for almost an hour and I cried like I was burying mother all over again. When I finally get home I stopped driving for a week. If I have to drive, I would find excuses why I could not go to places that would require me to drive a long distance. At times I would find myself reliving my fears all over again.

How was I supposed to care for my children living in fear and not going anywhere because I couldn't drive? I wanted to tell my family but I did not want my children to be split apart. I would pray, cry and ask God to deliver me from this stronghold. Over time my anxiety got worse. I tried counseling but it still had a hold on me. I prayed, "Lord, you said that you love me and you would remove this out of my life if I ask anything in Jesus' name."

I was in so much pain. I already could not process the loss of mother, now another thing added to my plate was anxiety. Where did this come from? How did this surface in my life? As a result of this, I tried to find love in a man that I thought I was in love with but pulled me away from my relationship with the Lord. When I began to date this man; we would go out on the weekends and I would find a babysitter for the children. I would never worry about what people thought because I was having fun and the pain was no longer there...at least I thought it was gone.

While dating him all those childhood fears and negative spirits began to surface. I thought about dancing but I didn't do this although I had the looks and the body. I knew I could make lots of money. This was the lie that satan was telling me. I was out doing what I wanted to do and I had strayed away from my upbringing, from the teaching of God's Word. Each year my soul was crying out for help because I knew this was not what I should be doing. But when you are afraid, hurt, and alone we tend to go back to a place of ease not wanting to deal with the facts. The fact was I knew that God had a special calling on my life in spite of all I had been through. I did not want and I was not going to let my stepfather's plan for my life become a reality. I kept on fighting, praying and trusting in the Word of God for my life although I was outside of His will doing what I wanted to do.

Many years passed and I broke off the bad relationship I was in but still I battled with anxiety for many years. Bound by my past fears, guilt, and shame I continued to seek God's will for my life. No matter how hard I tried I still had bad panic and anxiety attacks. The attacks had gotten so bad some days I would stay in the house all day.

It's really amazing how something can take control of your life only if you let it and this is what I had done. I allowed the anxiety to take over my life. I was not there for my children when they wanted to go certain places. How could I tell them, "Oh by the way, Mommy is afraid to go outside?" I would just say I did not feel good. I could not even drive around the corner to the store. If I would go to the store it would be at night. I was really bound.

Anxiety controls the mind and makes you feel like you are about to die or pass out, you cannot breathe, your heart races, you get nervous, you try to escape from being around others, and you try to isolate yourself from large crowds. What a frightening experience and sad way to live. I kept telling myself I have got to get control of this. I knew if I didn't, I could lose my children and they meant the world to me.

When I would go to church I would sit far in the back row so I could leave if I had an attack. Do you see how I had conditioned my mind and my thoughts to give in to my fears? I would read books, many books, regarding my sickness. Somehow I would find myself right back where I started and I just wanted to die. Many times I had thoughts about killing myself. I did not want to live like this. My mother was gone and I felt all alone, but wait what about my little babies? I had to live for them, no one in my family knew of this illness. I had lived this way for years and covered it up very well. My children acted out poorly in school but had good grades I knew it was my fault because of the way I was with them not able to give them the attention and support that was needed for school.

Each year that passed I missed mother more and more. I had to make up in my mind that she would not want me to live like this and this was not the way for me to raise her grandchildren. So I confronted anxiety in the face and knew it was a sign straight from hell. I teamed up with a support group from the church that I was attending and they provided counseling for anyone that wanted it, and I wanted and needed it badly. Each month I went I could see my strength getting stronger. The anxiety was still there but not as strong. Now, I was living life. I moved into my own place with my children, worked, and paid bills. I would found myself driving more and taking the kids to different places having family time, what a wonderful feeling.

Each morning I would drop the children off to school and go see my grandmother. One particular morning something was troubling my spirit and I rushed over to check on her. As I got closer to the house I became very nervous and did not know why. I rang the doorbell, no answered, I knocked on the door as hard as I could and still no answer. I then went to her bedroom and knocked on her bedroom window, no answer. I said to myself, "Please, let everything be okay."

The bedroom window was open where my old room was. I stuck my head in the window and called out for my grandmother, she still did not answer. I crawled in the bedroom only to smell smoke coming from underneath the door. I opened the bedroom door and the house was full of smoke. I turned my attention to the burning pot that was on the stove and began opening all the doors and windows in the house placing a wet rag over my mouth so I could find grandmother.

I ran all over searching and found her sleeping in her bed. I called her name and placed dashes of water over her face so that she would wake up. I put a robe on her and took her outside. I called 9-1-1 so that they could come and check her out to make sure there wasn't any smoke in her lungs. I could not imagine losing my grandmother. My mother was already gone and this would have pushed me over the edge.

In 1994, the kids were all asleep and I stayed up to watch the news because the weather was really bad. We were under a flash flood warning and in an effort to be prepared in case we had to evacuate I began packing clothes for myself and the kids to go to a shelter. When I walked outside the streets were already flooded. I went back inside and began to pray. The water started flooding the house and fear starting setting in. I woke the children up and told them to get dressed. We waited for someone to rescue us. While waiting the water began to rise higher and higher, it was waist high. The children began to scream "mommy please make it stop" I could not make the water stop and did the only thing I could think of to save them. I put a mattress on top of the kitchen table in order to get them up higher and out of the water. We were rescued and when I was able to return to my home I faced a very discouraging site. Everything in my home was destroyed. We lost everything material, but God had spared our lives.

Months passed and grandmother grew ill, which was a setback for me. She was placed in the hospital for observation. I went to see her every day. One night I received a phone call telling me that I should come to the hospital that she was about to leave to go home and be with the Lord. This news pulled me way down. I regressed right away. I went back into my shell and started having more and more panic attacks. I would cry all the time and stayed at home. I quit my job and lived off of my savings. I slept all day. I would get the kids ready for school and kiss them goodbye. I could barely walk outside to the end of the stairs to see them off to school. I was right where I was when I lost mother, now starting from the beginning all over again.

    We prepared for my grandmother's home going services. I was very sad and lost and I started dating a man that wasn't good for me and I knew it, but I didn't care. The woman that saved me from a horrible childhood was gone and I didn't know how to deal with all the pain. So I did what made me forget.

    The next few years of my life were very complex and hard. In one year, I lost my father, my son was diagnosed with Lupus; he was in and out of the hospital every year. I cried every night before I would go to bed but I must say through every negative doctor's report my son has remained hopeful and prayerful. Many days life would beat upon him really hard but one thing about him he never gives up. He has a very good outlook on his life. He applies the word of God to every negative doctor's report and keeps pressing and trusting in the Word of God.

    The next year my baby sister was almost taken

from me. I wanted to give up on life, my children were grown and the relationship that I had with my children wasn't the best. I thought they no longer needed me. I even asked God, "Why am I still here, I did not want to live like this everyone around me seems to be leaving. My spirit wanted to return back to being that scared hurt little girl. One day, I got up, looked myself in the mirror and remembered what my grandmother told me. "When the storms of life are really bad keep the faith and stop feeling sorry for yourself." My Aunt would always tell me, this too shall pass.

The Lord showed me His will for my life while I was drowning in self-pity. Each day I began to read and study God's word. I remember what my grandmother told me, "baby, that which does not kill you will make you strong". I knew that I was not dying and that I had to get out of my pity party. I purposed in my heart that I was strong and I had to be strong. Each day I would go to church my Pastor's lesson topic was tailor made just for me, so I kept going and applying the word to everything that I was going through and I began to see the hand of God move in my life. Now that my life is restored I shall have double. Thanks to God for Dr. Charles Perry Jr. and First Lady Charlette Perry, my spiritual parents.

CHAPTER SEVEN
-Living Free Now Restored-

In my final chapter I will cover all areas. Why? Because I want each person that reads this last chapter to break free and be healed from whatever it is that's on your heart? Ask the Savior to help, comfort, strengthen and heal you, He will see you through.

> RESTORED
> verb (used with object), re·stored, re·stor·ing.
> to bring back into existence, use, or the like; re-establish: to restore order.
> to bring back to a former, original, or normal condition, as a building, statue, or painting.
> to bring back to a state of health, soundness, or vigor.
> to put back to a former place, or to a former position, rank, etc.: to restore the king to his throne.
> to give back; make return or restitution of (anything taken away or lost).

Only God himself can restore our lives but we must put in the work and apply the Word of God to our lives and know that we will have the "VICTORY over defeat." Many years in my life I went through things that did not make sense to me, what I did not know was that it was not for me to make sense of. It was a learning experience to make me stronger. I didn't know it then my test would be a testimony for others. I'm not sure where you are in your life or where you would like to be, but no matter where you are or what you may go through find and imagine yourself being free from whatever it is. (a bad relationship that you need to let go of, an addiction, past mistakes, loved ones that have hurt or mistreated you, a relationship that has left you with pain, a bad doctors report, and even someone taking you for granted.)

They say the number seven is the sign of completion. Now that I am a restored woman, I can look back on my broken childhood with ease. There are moments I ask myself, "How did I ever make it through? I was exposed too soon, fearful, worried and abused. How did I ever endure living the nightmare of when it all began, preparing myself to run away to be safe, finding myself sixteen, married and pregnant, and trying not to repeat the cycle with all my hidden fears?" I kept telling myself one day that I will be free and restored.

I thank God for restoring me along with my spiritual leaders and the many prayers that my grandmother and my aunts who helped me to become the woman that I am today. Now the healing has come.

I can recall like it was just yesterday. I was sitting at home reading a book when I received a phone call from my sister telling me that my stepfather was in the hospital. I said I was not going to go see him, because of the things he had done to me. I told myself, "your healing is here, embrace it. It's time to let go and never look back on those bad experiences because they were things that happened in your past."

As I closed my eyes and began to pray to the Father, my prayer was, "Lord, please don't let me go back to my past. It's no longer part of my life."

I hung up the phone and I prayed again and asked God to be with me, comfort me and cover my mind, heart and emotions when I saw him. I asked God to give me the peace and the forgiveness that I would need to release in the atmosphere when I stepped into his room. I told my baby daughter what had happened to me and she said "Mother, you should go and see him because this will bring closure to all the hurt and pain that he did to you."

So, we drove to the hospital and as I walked to the front door of the hospital I began to pray again for strength when I saw him face to face. I stopped and asked the nurse where his room was and she told me. At first my daughter said she was going to stay outside because she was angry at what he had done to me. "I need you with me," I told her. "Because we are two and he is one."

What I really wanted to tell her was as Deuteronomy 32:30 explains to us; *if one can put a thousand enemies to flight, and two can put ten thousand enemies to flight, just imagine what we can do when we are together.* When two of you get together on anything at all on earth and make a prayer of it, my Father in Heaven goes into action. I knew that she would understand me telling her my way. When I got home I opened up the word of God to the book of Deuteronomy and explained to her what I was talking about that we are two and he is one. Two are more powerful than one in numbers.

When I opened the door there he laid on his bed of affliction in the hospital. Even before I went in the room I pictured him weak and frail on a breathing machine. For a moment my flesh rose up inside of me and wanted for this to be true. I wanted to give him the beat down he deserved from all the beatings that he gave my mother. I even thought about being the one to pull the plug! What an amazing God, He's so awesome because when I opened the door there he was…the man that inflicted so much pain and abuse in not only my life but in the lives of my family.

I began to thank God for His promise when He said, "I am the Lord that heals thee!" (Exodus 15:26 NIV) He allows us to go through certain things in our lives so that He may receive all the glory and make us strong. I never knew how strong I was until I was face to face with the man that abused me and my family for years. The one that caused me to live in guilt, shame, hurt, fear, anxiety, suicidal thoughts, panic attacks, loneliness, bitterness, always on edge, not truly understanding love and always on the defensive side. Yes, I was all of this in one person; you talk about multiple personalities, I was this person. The Lord showed me that even with all of those things I dealt with I did not have to go through a twelve-step program. That I had one word that was so powerful and could wipe away all I have been through and that word is, "Forgiveness."

You see, forgiveness is not for the other person it is for you. I forgave him so that I could be free. He looked me in my eyes and all he would say was that I fought him. No, he did not utter one word of apology. This was just fine with me because the Lord had already spoken to me and told me that I had been set free.

In 2010, I received the phone call that he had died. I was somewhat relieved and at the same time rejoicing because I no longer had to see him again. I received a call from my aunt who said to me "baby you are free, you don't have to worry about him ever again". I did attend the service and that was finally closure for me. All the years that passed from my childhood, my adolescence, young adult, and now that I am in my early fifties, God has brought me to a position that my only hope is in Him. I believe in His word.

I went home and cried out to God. I've had many leaders speak so many things over my life and God promised me that He would never leave me nor forsake me. He promised that He would be there when no one was there. I write to you to encourage you not to be locked up by your past. Let nothing ever put you in prison in your mind, soul, or your spirit where you have to lay in defeat and give up on your dreams. You are so much more than what has broken you. Let the love of Christ rule in your heart, because God did it for me and He will do it for you.

Now I am a member of a local church that teaches about restoring lives through the Word of God. It all makes sense to me now that in one's life we may not know the real reason why we go through what we go through, but it is at the end when it is really revealed to us and we have full knowledge and can understand. Then we are grateful for every mountain, every trial and every bad experience, because we know what it really means to press our way through. We can really grasp what it is to have faith, trust, and believe in God and the plans that He has for our lives.

I found myself thinking about the long process waiting for my healing while recovering from my past. As I began to talk to God I would pray and ask God to show me His Glory. I asked Him why I had so much pain at the end; it was like preparing for surgery. I guess one would say it's not the pre-op that really hurts it's the post-op. You have to deal with the scars and pain. This is a huge process of recovery because it will hurt so that the healing may come. I could not imagine ever wanting to go through what I went through ever again. I raised my children alone and each time someone died in my family I thought about how I was alone; but the Holy Spirit was so great and reminded me that he would never leave me. Don't think about the death of the situation think about the life of it and live life to its fullest.

I talked to many friends who shared their stories of heartache, pain, hurt, disappointment, and how they wanted to give up. Often times I would find myself forgetting about all that I was going through to be there for them. Not being able to fully live my life; afraid of what if's is not a healthily place for anyone. I know I had to make some really smart decisions on how to break this stronghold over my life. I worked hard so that my children would have a better life. I would work and work, then I redirected my career in a different way. I wanted to do more and become more. I enrolled in an interior-decorating program received my certification and focused my attention on event planning, but there was still something missing.

It was a nice Sunday morning and I was getting ready for church. There was something different about this Sunday. I arrived to the eight o'clock service. There was a special guest a prophet. He was teaching on, "Halfway There." As I sat and listened knowing where he was going with the message, I knew this was confirmation telling me not to give up and to learn how to trust in God for everything that I needed. He began to walk through the congregation speaking a word of prophecy over the lives of the members. I was sitting on the front row; he walked past me and then came back, and confirmed just what I was doing in my private time. So you see, when the Word of God is confirmed from a higher source, you must obey God's words.

I had been this way for many years and to imagine my life differently seemed to be out of my reach. I could see it, but could I really live my life free from my past? Every year I was a step closer to what seemed impossible for me. I would tell myself that I could not keep allowing something or someone that is no longer around me to control me for the rest of my life. While going through my pain and fears others would remind me, "just get over it, you are allowing this to take control of you because you won't let it go."

Well it is easier said than done. I did not know how to process it out of my life. I would have really bad days and then really good days. I suffered from depression for many years but I was able to continue on with my daily activities. Each step I took was a step closer than where I started. It is amazing when you are recovering from your past, your past will try and remind you that you are going backward and not forward. I had purposed in my heart that I was not going to allow my past to keep me from being what I dreamed to be, and the purpose of the wonderful life that God had for me to live. Being free is not just saying that you are free; you have to own it, embrace it, take control of it and not let go of the determination that you desire to be free.

Trusting and reading God's word helped me to make it through. I started reading spiritual books on how to pray effectively, and how to make the Lord the center of my life. I read the book of Proverbs that is full of wisdom. I read the book of Daniel that tells you about fasting and prayer. I asked God what His purpose for my life was and what was I supposed to be doing. As the days would go by I sought God's will for my life and for Him to show me His glory, because what I went through in my past life I wanted to channel all that pain into something that would be life rewarding. My desire is to give back to others that may be experiencing some of the issues I have gone through.

I started writing and the Holy Spirit visited me each day. At first it seemed like God answered me quickly and gave me very detailed instructions. As I followed the instructions, adversity tried to come but I stood on the word of God each and every day. This is what happens when you are focused on what you are called to do, the attack of the evil one. I looked beyond all of the attacks and did what the Holy Spirit told me to do. As the process of healing began, I found myself living at peace with everything by praying to God daily for his word to be made known in every situation that would arise. I was now in a place where I needed to be to hear from God.

I was broken, I was so many things but most importantly I was determined to make it, in spite of all the hell I went through not knowing how I was going to make it, but knowing the Lord would be able to bring me out. Sometimes it's in the middle of the ending of a thing when you first know that what did not kill you would make you strong. I am stronger now and I am no longer fearful. I am happy. I am complete in the Master. I love my life. I love the restored relationship that I have with my children.

I found that when you have a relationship with the father and you spend time with Him reading His word daily, fasting and praying there are no limits when it comes to GOD, because he is so faithful. Whether you have been raped, molested, beaten, have an addiction, live with anxiety, fear, depression, you have health issues, single mother, homeless, without a job, looking for love, angry, bitter, cannot let go of a love that has left you, finding love in the wrong someone, tired of people taking you for granted, hurting, cheating or being cheated on, trying to find your place in life or your purpose, lost someone dear to you, or overwhelmed with life. All those words are many, but there is one word that will take the place of them all and that word is, "RESTORED."

Do not allow the negative voices or the things that you have been through in your life keep you from reaching your dreams. You may have a slight detour or you may be redirected, but you will reach your destination. It's written that no matter where you find yourself in life you can do all things through Christ that strengthens you. Continue to read God's Word and it will lead and guide you into all truths. His Word can never lie. So as I end my chapter I would like to say to my readers. In God's words:

- There's love for any lack you may experience
- There's healing for any health issues you may experience.
- There's triumph in every tear you may cry.

- There's an angel watching over you in all areas of your life.
- There's miraculous power for your mistakes
- There's strength for your weakness
- There's faith for your failures
- There's help when you're hurting
- There's support for your sorrow
- There's consolation for confusion

I want you to close your eyes and look at the things that have been holding and pulling you down, take a deep breath and let it out, now begin to look and focus on your new life, the life that God has promised you.

BARBARA HILL-JACKSON

My prayer is this:

Father, I pray for every person that has read this book, "Broken Child Restored Woman."
I pray that in the midst of everything that is going on in their lives that you would help them to find peace, letting them know with you all things are possible if they only believe.
Lord, help them to find closure to all doors that must remain closed, while they begin to walk through new doors that you will open.
Letting go of all the past hurts and pain.
Lord, taking off the old and putting on the new in Christ Jesus,
Lord, I know that some may have lost their way, but I know that you are the compass when they lose their way.
Lord, I thank you for healing them, blessing them, taking every need that is on their heart and providing the need.
Lord, I thank you for giving them strength when they have lost a love one.
Lord thank you for your peace, love and your power through the difficult times they may be facing.
Lord, I trust in your word for their lives,
Lord, I know that you have restored their lives.
Give them all the resources that they will ever need to stay prayerful, hopeful, and most of all keeping their minds on you and you will keep them in perfect peace.
Lord let every man find his way to you; let every woman know their place in you.
Let every child remain hopeful for their hope is in you.
I pray for the leaders in this country and that you would guide their decisions.
I pray for those that are at war I ask that you would give them the desire to pursue peace at all times.
I pray for the man and woman of God that is the head of every worship center, church organization.

Bless them and keep them in perfect peace and place a double hedge of protection over them daily.
Last but not least Lord let the work that I do and all the words in all of my books that I write be pleasing and acceptable in your holy sight and may it heal, help and bless those that are hurting. More importantly let them know that you are their God and you would never leave them.......

In Jesus' Name, Amen

Love
Barbara

"Restored"
By Barbara Jackson

Now that I'm free and fully restored, I'm walking through every open door.

Goodbye fear because I've learned to trust again.
I put my faith in God and not mortal man.

I'm no longer hurt and filled with strife
I'm a restored woman that's highly favored and living my life.

Whether it was my pass that tried to keep me locked up you see
I'm a restored woman that has been set free

I'm living my life now at its best
I have endured and pressed my way through every trial and every test

I know what it means to patiently wait
Trusting God and to keep the faith.

I may have been broken and sometimes abused
The Lord fights my the battles, so therefore I never loose

I know my life has been hard and I have to fight to win
I keep pressing because in Christ Jesus I always win

Blessings, power and favor belong to me. I can now live my life fully restored and set free.

No longer will I ever worry again; being broken by life or love
Because I know The Lord; He's watching from above
"To God Be the Glory for the things that He has done in My Life.

-*About the Author*-

Ms. Barbara Jackson is a 51-year old single woman. Her passion is helping and encouraging others in the word of God. She seeks to find ways to make sure that everyone is happy and enjoying life. She often finds herself reaching out and encouraging those that she meets. She lives in Texas.

Barbara works full time in the healthcare industry. She is the owner of Sudie's Decor Wedding and Event Planning Service. She is also a proud member of Evan E. Worthing Sr. High School Alumni. Barbara is also a member of the BB Couture Woman's Group, FBCC Seeds of Faith Ministries, and Lupus Volunteer Foundation. Currently, Ms. Jackson is a member of the Word of Restoration International Church. Barbara often takes time out of her busy schedule to help support homeless shelters.

She spends each morning watching and listening to the word of God before she starts her day. She enjoys reading self-motivational books. She also seeks ways to enrich her life and encourage others.

While her past has not always been the best, she uses it as a stepping-stone to build and climb to find ways to help others overcome some of the same things that she has gone through. This author, businesswoman, mother of three, will continue to seek ways and find resources that are available to build a platform to inspire women to push past their pain and grab hold to their beliefs so that they may obtain their dreams. Her three children, Kriscynthia, Shammie Jr. and Emma are the love of her life, and she could not imagine her life without them.

Question - Why Did I Stay?

Now that I am restored, I often ask myself this question, "Why did you stay?"

I stayed out of LOVE for my mother. I wanted to protect her from this evil man, although mother couldn't see this but as a child I could. I watched him tear our family apart, move us from place to place. My mother, sister, brother and I were very happy all we had was each other. This man came into our lives and took all this away. He brought a life filled with drugs, wild parties, stress, confusion, pain and abuse into our family. Each time I would get up the courage to leave, the love for my mother kept me from leaving.

Over and over again I reminded myself, "Who will be there to protect mother if I leave?" You see, throughout my book I shared with you that I was the strongest in the family. Each time that I wouldn't allow him to sexually abuse me he would beat mother. Oftentimes I would come home to mother screaming with him beating her never fighting him back. The older I became, I realized that I had to protect her by going and standing in between them, he knew that I wasn't afraid of him. Every day the beatings grew worse, I would talk to mother and try to convince her to leave but never did she listen, so I stayed until one day I just couldn't take the abuse any longer.

I purposed in my heart all of the abuse was not really worth me staying if mother couldn't see that this man would kill her or one of us. Yes, I stayed much too long, but as a child I didn't know how to leave. How do you leave someone so fragile and that you love dearly? As a young girl I watched mother one year try to take her own life because of the pain and abuse, so how could I leave a woman that was so frail, weak. I thought it would be my fault if something bad happened to her.

Mother meant the world to me and to leave someone that I loved dearly would haunt me for my entire life. One day I had a long talk with mother and I shared with her what he was doing to me. I told her on so many times, yet she still did not believe me. I said, "Mother, I want you to listen to me step dad has been having me do things to him, he would make me perform oral sex on him and held a gun to my head, showed me nude photos, and made me watch nude movies with him, he put his penis inside of me, I started screaming and he stopped. Then the next night when you were at work he came into my room and did the very same thing night after night."

Mother looked at me as if I was lying and her response was, "Why are you telling me this? All you want to do is to stay home with him anyway."

This made me cry and I knew it was time for me to leave, my heart dropped. I called my godmother and told her that I wanted to live with grandmother. I told her my plans and she told me to be careful. So talking with mother her response helped me make my decision to leave and never did I think about changing my mind. If mother wanted to stay then I had to accept her decision to stay, but I left, and my life was so much better.

There was a lot of work to be done, because of the many years of abuse that I went through, but my grandmother held on to me and nurtured me, took me to church, loved me through all the pain, hurt and abuse. So parents, listen to your children, pay close attention to them and their behavior. You will see the real truth in the way that they behave. Don't ever allow anyone or anything come between you and your family, because one thing I know is that God honors families and we should protect our children at all cost, no matter what. Please listen to your child(ren).

NOTES

NOTES

BARBARA HILL-JACKSON

BROKEN CHILD RESTORED WOMAN

www.ingramcontent.com/pod-product-compliance
Lightning Source LLC
Chambersburg PA
CBHW060359050426
42449CB00009B/1819